Letters to the Thessalonians

By

WILLIAM MACDONALD

WALTERICK PUBLISHERS
P. O. Box 2216
Kansas City, Kansas 66110

TABLE OF CONTENTS

PAGE

Preface 5

1 Thessalonians

Introduction 9

Chapter 1 11

Chapter 2 21

Chapter 3 39

Chapter 4 46

Chapter 5 61

2 Thessalonians

Introduction 80

Chapter 1 81

Chapter 2 92

Chapter 3 105

Conclusion 113

Bibliography 132

PREFACE

In this commentary we adopt the following chronology of future events because we believe that it best harmonizes with the entire body of Scriptures.

1. First the rapture, that is, the coming of Christ for His saints. He comes to the air, the dead in Christ are raised, living believers are changed, and all go to the Father's house. This could take place at any moment, and will take place in a moment of time. The principal references to the rapture are John 14:1-4; 1 Corinthians 15:23,51-54; Philippians 3:20,21; 1 Thessalonians 1:10; 4:13-18; 2 Thessalonians 2:1; Hebrews 9:28; 10:37; James 5:7-9; 1 John 2:28; 3:2; Revelation 22:7,20.

2. Following the rapture, two important events will take place in heaven: the judgment seat of Christ and the marriage supper of the Lamb. The believer's works will be reviewed at the judgment seat of Christ, and he will be rewarded or suffer loss (Rom. 14:10-12; 1 Cor. 3:11-15; 2 Cor. 5:10; 2 Tim. 4:7,8). The marriage supper of the Lamb will celebrate the glorification of the church as the bride of the Lamb (Rev. 19:1-9).

3. Following the rapture, the earth faces a time known as the tribulation period. It may not start immediately after the rapture; there may be an interim period during which there will be a world-wide apostasy, a false

messiah known as the man of lawlessness will be revealed, and the temple will be rebuilt in Jerusalem (2 Thess. 2:1-4).

The tribulation itself will be a period of approximately seven years (the seventieth week of Daniel's prophecy) during which God will pour out judgments of ever-increasing intensity upon the earth (Dan. 9:27; Matt. 24:4-28; Rev. 6–19). The last half of the period is known as the great tribulation; it will witness distress and disasters of unprecedented severity (Matt. 24:15-31).

The tribulation marks the beginning of a longer period of time known as the day of the Lord when God directly intervenes in the affairs of the world, primarily with regard to the nation of Israel, but also in reference to the Gentile nations (Ezek. 30:1-5; Joel 2:1-11; 1 Thess. 5:1-3; 2 Thess. 2:2, ASV). The day of the Lord extends to the end of this world's history (2 Pet. 3:10).

4. Toward the end of the great tribulation, the Lord Jesus will return from heaven to earth to destroy His enemies and to inaugurate His millennial kingdom (Zech. 14:4; Mal. 4:1-3; Matt. 24:3,27,30,37,39; Acts 1:11; 1 Thess. 3:13; 2 Thess. 1:7-9; 2:8; Jude 14; Rev. 1:7; 19:11-16). All Old Testament references and most New Testament references to Christ's second advent deal with this event.

5. The 1000-year reign of Christ on earth will be an era of peace and prosperity (Isa. 2:4; Amos 9:13-15). He will reign with Jerusalem as His capital (Isa. 2:2,3; Jer. 3:17; Zech. 14:10,17,18), the church as His bride (Rev. 20:4; 21:9-27; 22:1-5), and Israel as His principal subjects (Deut. 28:13; Zech. 8:3,10-13), though Gentiles will also share in the blessings of His kingdom. It will be a time of fertility, longevity, and equity (Isa. 32:1; 35:1-7; 65:17-25; Rev. 20:4).

6. Following Christ's kingdom, Satan will be cast into the lake of fire (Rev. 20:10), the heavens and the earth will be destroyed by fire (2 Pet. 3:7-13), and the wicked dead will receive their final doom at the judgment of the great white throne (Rev. 20:11-15).

7. The final chapter is the eternal state, consisting of new heavens and a new earth (Rev. 21:1).

Not all Christians will agree with this chronology. There are numerous other viewpoints. And quite frankly there are difficulties no matter which viewpoint you hold. It is the nature of prophecy to be clear as to the major facts but not always clear on details until the events transpire.

So we offer this interpretation not as the final word but as a point of departure. It will give the student an outline of coming events. He can start with this and reject or modify it as he feels necessary from his own private study of the Word.

NOTE: All Scripture quotations are from the American Standard Version (ASV) unless otherwise indicated.

FIRST THESSALONIANS

INTRODUCTION

It was during Paul's second missionary journey that the light of the gospel first broke in upon the darkness of Thessalonica (Acts 17:1-10). Here is how it happened:

After Paul and Silas had been released from jail in Philippi, they traveled to Thessalonica via Amphipolis and Apollonia. Thessalonica at that time was a strategic city, both commercially and politically. True to form Paul went to the Jewish synagogue and showed from the Old Testament that the Messiah had to suffer and rise from the dead. He then went on to declare that Jesus of Nazareth was the promised Messiah. That lasted for three Saturdays. Some of the Jews were convinced, and took their place with Paul and Silas as Christian believers. Also, many of the Greek proselytes and quite a few of the leading women of the city were converted. Then the backlash started. The unbelieving Jews rounded up some of the hoodlums from the marketplace, incited a riot, and besieged the house of Jason where Paul and Silas had been staying. When they didn't find the preachers in the house, they dragged Jason and some of the other believers before the city rulers (politarchs), accusing them of having turned the world upside down. It was an unintended compliment. Then they charged the Christians with plotting the overthrow of Caesar by promoting another king named Jesus. The politarchs were troubled. They required Jason and his colleagues to post bail, probably adding strict orders for his guests to get out of town. Then Jason and the others were released.

The Christian brothers in Thessalonica decided that it would be wise for the preachers to leave town, so they sent them by night to Berea.

The remarkable thing is that when Paul and Silas departed, they left behind a local assembly of believers who were instructed in the doctrines of faith and who were unmoved by the persecution they endured. It would be easy to conclude from Acts 17:2 that Paul and his companions were in Thessalonica for only three Sabbaths. However, that may have been only the duration of their teaching ministry *in the synagogue*. Some suggest that Paul and his team may have spent as long as three months in the city. The apostle's letters to them show that the Thessalonians had a broad acquaintance with Christian doctrine, and they could scarcely have received this in three or four weeks.

From Berea Paul went to Athens (Acts 17:15). There he heard that the believers in Thessalonica were being persecuted. He tried to visit them, but Satan hindered (1 Thess. 2:17,18), so he sent Timothy to them (3:1,2). Timothy brought back a report that was, on the whole, encouraging (3:6-8), and this prompted the apostle to write this letter. In it, he defends his ministry against slanderous attacks; he calls for separation from the prevailing immorality of that culture; he corrects misapprehensions about those who had died in Christ; he rebukes those who had quit working in view of Christ's coming; and he urges the saints to respect their spiritual leaders.

This is probably the first book of the New Testament to be written, and certainly the first of Paul's letters. It is generally dated AD 50-51, placing it within 20 years of the resurrection and ascension of the Lord Jesus.

One of the most important themes of 1 Thessalonians is the return of the Lord Jesus. It is mentioned at least once in each of the five chapters. G. R. Harding Wood put these references together and came up with the following excellent outline:

The Christian who is expecting the return of the Lord Jesus has no room for:

1. Idols in his heart (1:9,10)
2. Slackness in his service (2:9,19)
3. Divisions in his fellowship (3:12,13)
4. Depression in his mind (4:13-18)
5. Sin in his life (5:23)

1

I. INTRODUCTION (1:1)
  A. **The author and his associates (v. 1a):** Paul, and
     Silvanus, and Timothy
  B. **The persons addressed (v. 1b):** unto the church
    1. **Geographical designation:** of the Thessalo-
       nians
    2. **Spiritual position:** in God the Father and the
       Lord Jesus Christ
  C. **The greeting (v. 1c):** Grace to you and peace

1:1 The letter opens with the names of three men who
had been accused of turning the world upside down. The
charge was intended as a slander; it was actually a tribute.

Paul was the author of the letter. Silvanus and Timothy
were traveling with him at the time, so he included their
names. Silvanus is the same as Silas, the one who had sung
a duet with Paul in the prison at Philippi (Acts 16:25).
Timothy is the young brother from Lystra who had joined
Paul just before the trip to Thessalonica (Acts 16:1).

The letter was written to the church of the Thessalonians
in God the Father and the Lord Jesus Christ. The word
church was used at that time to describe any kind of an
assembly, so Paul wants to make it clear that this is not a
heathen assembly but one that is related to God as Father
and Jesus Christ as Lord.

The greeting "grace . . . and peace" embraces the best

11

blessings that anyone could enjoy on this side of heaven.
Grace is God's undeserved favor in every aspect of our
lives. Peace is the unruffled quietness which defies the
crashing, crushing circumstances of life. Grace is the cause
and peace the effect.

II. PAUL'S INTEREST IN THE SAINTS (1:2,3)
   ### A. His gratitude for them (v. 2a): We give thanks
   to God always for you all
   ### B. His prayers for them (v. 2b): making mention
   of you in our prayers
   ### C. His constant remembrance of them (v. 3): remembering without ceasing
   #### 1. The virtues remembered
      a) **Faith:** your work of faith
      b) **Love:** and labor of love
      c) **Hope:** and patience of hope in our Lord
      Jesus Christ
   #### 2. The place of remembrance: before our God
   and Father

1:2 Whenever Paul prayed he mentioned the Thessalonians. (Are we as faithful in remembering our Christian
brothers?) And it was always with thanksgiving that he
prayed for them, as he thought of their work of faith, their
labor of love, and their patience of hope.

1:3 Their work of faith probably refers primarily to
their conversion to God. This description of faith as a work
reminds us of the time when some of the people asked
Jesus, "What shall we do, that we might work the works of
God?" Jesus answered and said to them, "This is the work
of God, that ye believe on him whom he hath sent" (John
6:28,29). In this sense, faith is an act or deed. But it is not
toil by which a man earns merit or in which he can boast. In
fact, it is the only work that man can perform without
robbing Christ of His glory as Savior and without denying
his own status as a helpless sinner. Faith is a non-

meritorious work by which the creature acknowledges his Creator and the sinner acknowledges his Savior. Of course the expression "work of faith" also includes the life of faith which follows conversion.

In addition to their work of faith, Paul remembered their labor of love. This speaks, of course, of their service for God motivated by love to the Lord Jesus. Christianity is not a life to be endured for duty's sake, but a Person to be served for love's sake. To be His slave is perfect freedom, and "love for Him makes drudgery divine." Compared to love, the profit motive is a cheap, tawdry inducement. Love for Christ draws forth service that the dollar would never inspire. The Thessalonians were living testimonies to this fact.

Finally, Paul was thankful for their patience of hope. This speaks of their steadfast waiting for Jesus. They had been undergoing persecution as a result of their valiant stand for Christ. But no cracks had appeared in what Phillips calls their "sheer dogged endurance."

The place of remembrance is indicated by the phrase "before our God and Father." As Paul entered the presence of God in prayer, he rehearsed the spiritual birth and growth of the saints and breathed out his thanksgiving for their faith, love, and hope.

III. PAUL'S ASSURANCE CONCERNING THE SAINTS (1:4,5a): knowing, brethren beloved of God
A. The assured fact (v. 4): your election
B. The basis for this assurance (v. 5a)
  1. The negative side: how that our gospel came not unto you in word only
  2. The positive side
    a) The forcefulness: but also in power
    b) The agent: and in the Holy Spirit
    c) The effect: and in much assurance

1:4 The apostle was assured that these saints had been

13

chosen by God before the foundation of the world. But how did he know? Did he have some supernatural insight? No, he knew they were among the elect by the way they had received the gospel.

The doctrine of election teaches that God chose certain people in Christ before the foundation of the world (Eph. 1:4). It does *not* teach that He chose some to be damned. If men are finally lost, it is because of their own sin and unbelief.

The same Bible that teaches election also teaches human responsibility or man's free will. God makes a *bona fide* offer of salvation to all people everywhere. Whoever comes to Christ will find a warm welcome.

These two doctrines, election and free will, create an irreconcilable conflict in the human mind. But the Bible teaches both and so we should believe both even if we can't harmonize them.

We do not know who the elect are, and so we should carry the gospel to all the world. Sinners should not use the doctrine of election as an excuse for not believing. If they will repent and believe on the Lord Jesus Christ, God will save them.

1:5a When Paul says "our gospel," he does not imply a different message from that of the other apostles. The contents were the same; the difference was in the messengers.

The Thessalonians had not treated the message as a mere religious lecture; they had, of course, received it in word, but not in word only.

It came to them in power, and in the Holy Spirit, and in much assurance.

1. *In power*. The message worked in their lives with supernatural energy, producing conviction of sin, repentance, and conversion.
2. *In the Holy Spirit*. This power was produced by the Holy Spirit.
3. *In much assurance*. Paul preached with great confidence in the message. The Thessalonians accepted it

with much assurance as the word of God. The result in
their lives was full assurance of faith.

IV. **THE PROCESS BY WHICH THE THESSALO-
NIANS BECAME REPRODUCING CHRIS-
TIANS (1:5b-10)**
   A. **The exemplary lives of Paul and his companions (v. 5b):** even as ye know what manner of
   men we showed ourselves toward you for your
   sake
   B. **The transformed lives of the Thessalonians
   (v. 6)**
      1. **The models they copied:** And ye became im-
      itators of us, and of the Lord
      2. **The behavior imitated:** having received the
      word
         a) **Tribulation:** in much affliction
         b) **Jubilation:** with joy of the Holy Spirit.
   C. **The first sphere of their influence (v. 7):** so that
   ye became an ensample to all that believe in
   Macedonia and in Achaia
   D. **The widening circle of their testimony (vv. 8-
   10)**
      1. **The local source (v. 8a):** For from you
      2. **The active proclamation (v. 8b):** hath sound-
      ed forth
      3. **The glorious subject (v. 8c):** the word of the
      Lord
      4. **The immediate area (v. 8d):** not only in
      Macedonia and Achaia
      5. **The wider coverage (v. 8e):** but in every
      place
      6. **The resulting testimony (vv. 8f-10):** your
      faith to Godward is gone forth
         a) **Apostolic report unnecessary (v. 8g):** so
         that we need not to speak anything
         b) **The report of the new believers (vv.**

15

9,10): For they themselves report concerning us
- **(1) Reception (v. 9a):** what manner of entering in we had unto you
- **(2) Conversion (v. 9b):** and how ye turned unto God from idols
- **(3) Ministration (v. 9c):** to serve a living and true God
- **(4) Expectation (v. 10):** and to wait
  - **(a) The person:** for his Son
  - **(b) The place:** from heaven
  - **(c) The pledge:** whom he raised from the dead
  - **(d) The precious name:** even Jesus
  - **(e) The prospect:** who delivereth us from the wrath to come

1:5b Paul now reminds them of his own conduct while he was with them. He not only preached the gospel, but lived a consistent life. "The best sermon is a holy life."

1:6 Thus he could say, "Ye became imitators of us, and of the Lord." You would have expected him to say "of the Lord and of us," mentioning the Lord first. But here he is giving the order of their experience. Their first introduction to the Lord Jesus was in the life of the apostle.

It is sobering to think that people are supposed to be able to see Christ in us. The recurring challenge to our hearts is this:

> If perhaps of Christ their only view
> May be what they see of Him in you—
> Christian, what do they see?

We should be able to say with Paul, "Be imitators of me, just as I also am of Christ" (1 Cor. 11:1).

Notice that they received the word with affliction and joy. This is how they had imitated the Lord and the apostles. Externally there was affliction, internally there was joy. It is an unusual combination! For the man of the world, it is impossible to experience joy and affliction simultaneously; to him, sorrow is the opposite of joy. The Christian has a joy of the Holy Spirit that is independent of circumstances; to him, the opposite of joy is sin.

The affliction they endured was the persecution which followed their conversion.

1:7 The Thessalonians became model Christians. First of all, their example of joy in the midst of persecution was an example to believers in Macedonia and Achaia, that is, to all the Christians in Greece.

1:8 But their testimony didn't stop there. They became reproducing Christians. Like ripples in a pool, the word of the Lord spread out in ever-widening circles, first in Macedonia and Achaia, then in more distant places. Soon the news of their faith in God became so widespread that Paul didn't have to speak about it; the people already knew.

We are not intended to be terminals of our blessings, but channels through which they can flow to others. God shines in our hearts so that the light might shine out to others (2 Cor. 4:6, JND). If we have really drunk the water of salvation, then rivers of living water will flow forth to those around us (John 7:37,38).

1:9 It was a matter of common conversation that when the apostle and his colleagues went to Thessalonica, they had received a royal welcome. ". . . what a welcome we had among you" (RSV). Also it had become a matter of common knowledge that a startling transformation had taken place in the lives of many of the people. They had turned to God from their pagan idols and had yielded their will to God as bondslaves.

Notice that they turned to God from idols, not from idols to God. It wasn't that they had become fed up with their idols and then decided to give God a chance. No, they

17

turned to God and found Him so satisfying that they dropped their idols.

> 'Tis that look that melted Peter,
> 'Tis that face that Stephen saw,
> 'Tis that heart that wept with Mary,
> Can alone from idols draw.

Let us never lose the sense of thrill and awe that is implicit in this account. Two men go into a heathen city with the word of the Lord. They preach the gospel in the power of the Spirit. The miracle of regeneration takes place; men and women become so enraptured with the Savior that they abandon their idols. Next you have a local assembly of believers, praising God, living lives of holiness, bravely enduring persecution, and winning others to Christ. Truly the Lord's service is the prince of callings.

1:10 Not only were the Thessalonians serving the living and true God (in contrast to idols which are lifeless and false); they were waiting for the Lord Jesus. Notice the details of their expectation:

1. The Person—his Son
2. The Place—from heaven
3. The Pledge—whom he raised from the dead
4. The Precious Name—even Jesus
5. The Prospect—who delivereth us from the wrath to come

Thus we have in verses 9 and 10 the three aspects of the Thessalonians' experience:

> Turning (compare work of faith, v. 3)
> Serving (compare labor of love, v. 3)
> Waiting (compare patience of hope, v. 3)

G. R. Harding Wood analyzes them as follows:

Turning—looking to God
Serving—looking on the fields
Waiting—looking for Jesus

The Thessalonians were waiting for God's Son from heaven. This implies the possibility of His coming during their lifetime; in fact, at any moment during their lifetime. The imminent return of the Lord Jesus is the hope of the Christian. It is found in many passages of the New Testament, of which the following are a few:

Luke 12:36—"And be ye yourselves like unto men looking for their lord."

Romans 8:23—". . . we . . . waiting for our adoption, to wit, the redemption of our body."

1 Corinthians 11:26—"For as often as ye eat this bread, and drink the cup, ye proclaim the Lord's death till he come."

2 Corinthians 5:2—"For verily in this we groan, longing to be clothed upon with our habitation which is from heaven."

Galatians 5:5—"For we through the Spirit by faith wait for the hope of righteousness."

Philippians 3:20,21—". . . we wait for a Saviour, the Lord Jesus Christ."

Philippians 4:5—". . . The Lord is at hand."

Titus 2:13—"Looking for the blessed hope and appearing of the glory of the great God and our Saviour Jesus Christ."

Hebrews 9:28—"Christ . . . shall appear a second time, apart from sin, to them that wait for him, unto salvation."

Hebrews 10:37—"For yet a very little while, He that cometh shall come, and shall not tarry."

James 5:7-9—"Be patient therefore, brethren, until the coming of the Lord . . . the coming of the Lord is at hand . . . the judge standeth before the doors."

1 Peter 4:7—"But the end of all things is at hand."

1 John 3:3—"And every one that hath this hope set on him purifieth himself, even as he is pure."

Jude 21—". . . looking for the mercy of our Lord Jesus Christ unto eternal life."

Revelation 3:11—"I come quickly."

Revelation 22:7—"And behold, I come quickly. . . ."

Revelation 22:12—"Behold, I come quickly. . . ."

Revelation 22:20—". . . Yea; I come quickly. Amen: come, Lord Jesus."

The Christian knows that he may be required to pass through death, but he also knows that the Lord may come momentarily and that, in that event, he will enter heaven without dying.

No prophecy of the Scripture needs to be fulfilled before the coming of Christ for His people. It is the next great event in God's program.

We cannot be looking momentarily for the Lord's return if some event or period of time has to intervene. The pre-tribulation rapture position is the only one that permits the believer to look for Christ's coming today. Other views force abandonment of the imminency of His return.

The One we look for is Jesus, *our Deliverer from the wrath to come*. This description of the coming Savior may be understood in two ways:

1. He delivers us from the eternal punishment of our sins. On the cross He endured the wrath of God against our sins. Through faith in Him, we have the value of His work reckoned to our account. Henceforth there is no condemnation for us because we are in Christ Jesus (Rom. 8:1).

2. But He also delivers us from the coming period of judgment when the wrath of God will be poured out on the world that has rejected His Son. This period is known as the tribulation and the time of Jacob's trouble. It is described in Daniel 9:27; Matthew 24:4-28; 1

Thessalonians 5:1-11; 2 Thessalonians 2:1-12; Revelation 6:1—19:10.

2

V. REVIEW OF PAUL'S MINISTRY, MESSAGE, AND CONDUCT AT THESSALONICA (2:1-12)

A. His ministry was (vv. 1,2)
1. **Successful (v. 1):** For yourselves, brethren, know our entering in unto you, that it hath not been found vain
2. **Courageous (v. 2)**
   a) **It followed his persecution at Philippi:** but having suffered before and been shamefully treated, as ye know, at Philippi
   b) **It was accompanied by opposition in Thessalonica:** we waxed bold in our God to speak unto you the gospel of God in much conflict

B. His message was (v. 3)
1. **True as to its source:** For our exhortation is not of error
2. **Pure as to its motive:** nor of uncleanness
3. **Dependable as to its method:** nor in guile

C. His ministry was a sacred stewardship (v. 4)
1. **Its source:** but even as we have been approved of God
2. **Its message:** to be intrusted with the gospel
3. **Its motive:** so we speak; not as pleasing men, but God who proveth our hearts

D. His behavior was (vv. 5-12)
1. **Unhypocritical (v. 5a):** For neither at any time were we found using words of flattery, as ye know
2. **Undisguised (v. 5b):** nor a cloak of covet-

21

ousness, God is witness
3. **Undemanding (v. 6)**
   a) **A noble refusal:** nor seeking glory of men, neither from you nor from others
   b) **A legitimate privilege:** when we might have claimed authority as apostles of Christ
4. **Gentle (v. 7)**
   a) **A true observation:** But we were gentle in the midst of you
   b) **A helpful illustration:** as when a nurse cherisheth her own children
5. **Affectionate (v. 8a):** even so, being affectionately desirous of you
6. **Sacrificial (v. 8b)**
   a) **The expected readiness:** we were well pleased to impart unto you, not the gospel of God only
   b) **The unexpected willingness:** but also our own souls
   c) **The impelling reason:** because ye were become very dear to us
7. **Industrious (v. 9a):** For ye remember, brethren, our labor and travail
8. **Tireless (v. 9b):** working night and day
9. **Self-supporting (v. 9c):** that we might not burden any of you
10. **Evangelistic (v. 9d):** we preached unto you the gospel of God
11. **Holy (v. 10a):** Ye are witnesses, and God also, how holily
12. **Righteous (v. 10b):** and righteously
13. **Blameless (v. 10c):** and unblameably we behaved ourselves toward you that believe
14. **Fatherly (vv. 11,12)**
   a) **The forms of parental instruction (v. 11):** as ye know how we dealt with each one of you, as a father with his own children, exhorting you, and encouraging

you, and testifying

b) **The goal in view (v. 12):** to the end that ye should walk worthily of God, who calleth you into his own kingdom and glory

2:1 In the latter part of 1:5, the apostle had briefly alluded to his personal character and conduct while he was at Thessalonica. Now he launches into a more thorough review of his ministry, message, and behavior.

The point here, of course, is that the primary ministry of a Christian is the ministry of character. What we are is far more important than anything we ever say. Our unconscious influence speaks more loudly than our conscious influence.

As Dr. Denney has said, "A Christian's character is the whole capital he has for carrying on his business. In most other callings, a man may go on, no matter what his character is, provided his balance at the bank is on the right side; but a Christian who has lost his character has lost everything."

Jim Elliot wrote in his journal, "In spiritual work, if nowhere else, the character of the worker decides the quality of his work. Shelley and Byron may be moral freelancers and still write good poetry. Wagner may be lecherous and still produce fine music, but it cannot be so in any work for God. Paul could refer to his own character and manner of living for proof of what he was saying to the Thessalonians. Nine times over in this first epistle he says, 'you know,' referring to the Thessalonians' firsthand observation of Paul's private as well as public life. Paul went to Thessalonica and lived a life that more than illustrated what he preached; it went beyond illustration to convincing proof. No wonder so much work in the Kingdom today is shoddy; look at the moral character of the worker."[1]

Perhaps in these verses the apostle is defending himself against the false accusation of his critics. At any rate, he first reminds the Thessalonians that his ministry was successful. They themselves were living evidence that his work had been fruitful. They knew that his visit was not a failure. They themselves had been converted and an assembly had been established.

2:2 Then too his ministry was courageous. The bitter opposition and outrageous treatment at Philippi, including his imprisonment there with Silas, did not daunt, discourage, or intimidate him. He pressed on to Thessalonica. There with the courage which only God can give, he preached the gospel in the face of continued conflict. A less robust person could have thought of numerous theological reasons why God was calling him to more congenial audiences. But not Paul! He preached the message fearlessly despite great opposition, a direct result of the Spirit's filling.

2:3 The apostle's exhortation to believe the gospel was true as to its source, pure as to its motive, and dependable as to its method. As to its source, it did not spring from false doctrine but from the truth of God. As to its motive, the apostle looked on the Thessalonians unselfishly, with their good in view, and not with any ulterior, impure desire. As to its method, there was no clever plot to deceive them. Apparently his jealous enemies were accusing him of heresy, lustful desire, and craftiness.

2:4 To Paul the ministry was a sacred stewardship. He was the steward, approved by God, and the gospel was the precious treasure that had been entrusted to him by God. His responsibility was to please God by the faithful proclamation of the message, no matter what man's reaction might be. It was clear to him that he couldn't please both God and man, so he chose to please God, who tests our hearts and then rewards accordingly.

A steward is obligated to please the one who pays him. Preachers may sometimes be tempted to hold back the full truth for fear of repercussion from those who contribute to

24

their support. But God is the Master, and He knows when the message is watered down or suppressed.

2:5 In verses 5-12 Paul gives an account of his behavior at Thessalonica; in doing so, he has left a splendid pattern for all servants of Jesus Christ.

First of all, he never stooped to flattery or insincerity in order to achieve results. His words were honest and transparent, and his motives were free from hypocrisy.

Secondly, he never used the work of the Lord as a cloak under which he could hide a selfish desire to get rich. His service was not a false front for a covetous heart.

To disprove any charge of flattery, he appeals to the saints. But to disprove any thought of covetousness, he appeals to God, Who is the only One Who can read the heart.

2:6 Here we have another impressive insight into the character of this great man of God. As apostles of Christ, he and his colleagues were entitled to financial support (here called "glory") from the Thessalonians. But they were determined that they would not be burdensome to them, so they worked day and night to provide for their own needs. It was a different story in Corinth. There Paul worked so as not to give his critics any ground for accusing him of preaching for money. In Thessalonica he worked because the saints were poor and persecuted, and he did not want to be an added burden to them.

2:7 Instead of lording it over God's heritage, he was gentle among them as a nursing mother. The word "nurse" here does not mean a Registered Nurse caring for the sick, but a mother caring for her own children. Paul realized that new converts need nursing, and he carried on this ministry with all the solicitude of a devoted mother.

2:8 So deep was his affectionate concern for them, he was anxious to share with them rather than to receive from them. His was not a cold, perfunctory dispensing of the gospel but a pouring out of his very soul. He loved them, and love is careless of cost. Like his Master, he did not come to be served, but to serve and to give his life (Mark 10:45).

2:9 A further evidence of Paul's unselfishness is here: we see him working as a tentmaker in order to earn a living so that he could minister to the people without being a burden to them. While it is true that the gospel preacher is entitled to financial support from other Christians, it is commendable to see him foregoing this right, if necessary, from time to time. A true minister of Christ will continue to preach the gospel whether he receives money for it or has to work to finance himself. Notice the expressions "labor and travail" and "night and day." They speak of toil and drudgery at all hours of the day and night. The gospel didn't cost the Thessalonians a cent, but it cost the apostle plenty.

2:10 The believers could testify to Paul's exemplary behavior toward them; and God also was a Witness that he was holy, righteous, and unblameable. Holy, that is, separated to God from sin. Righteous in character and in conduct. Unblameable toward God and man.

If the best sermon is a holy life, Paul was a great preacher. Not like another preacher whose eloquence was greater than his conduct: when he was in the pulpit, the people wished he would never leave it, but when he was out of it, they wished he would never enter it again.

2:11 In verse 7, he had compared himself to a nursing mother; now he changes the figure to that of a devoted father. If the former suggests tenderness and affection, the latter suggests wisdom and counsel. As a father, he exhorted them to live a holy life, he encouraged them to go on for the Lord in spite of persecutions, and he testified concerning the blessedness of obedience to the will and word of God.

2:12 The goal of his ministry was that the saints might walk worthily of God Who had called them to His own kingdom and glory.

In ourselves we are unworthy of God or of a place in heaven; the only worthiness we have is found in the Lord Jesus Christ. But as sons of God, we are expected to walk worthily of the high calling; this we can do by submitting ourselves to the control of the Holy Spirit and by confessing and forsaking sin in our lives continually.

All who are saved are subjects of the kingdom of God. At the present time that kingdom is invisible, and the King is absent. But the moral and ethical teachings of the kingdom apply to us today. When the Lord Jesus returns to reign, the kingdom will then be set up in visible form, and we will share the glory of the King in that day.

VI. REVIEW OF THE THESSALONIANS' RESPONSE TO THE GOSPEL (2:13-16)

A. The apostle's thanksgiving for the way they received the message (v. 13): And for this cause we also thank God without ceasing, that, when ye received from us the word of the message, even the word of God

1. **What the message is not:** ye accepted it not as the word of men
2. **What the message is**
   a) **Divine:** but, as it is in truth, the word of God
   b) **Effective:** which also worketh in you that believe

B. The persecutions endured by the Thessalonians (vv. 14-16)

1. **The examples they followed (v. 14a):** For ye, brethren, became imitators of the churches of God which are in Judaea in Christ Jesus
2. **The identity of their persecutors (v. 14b):** for ye also suffered the same things of your own countrymen

3. **The persecutors of the Judaean Christians (vv. 14c-16):** even as they did of the Jews
   a) **Their treatment of Christ (v. 15a):** who both killed the Lord Jesus
   b) **Their treatment of the prophets (v. 15b):** and the prophets
   c) **Their treatment of Paul (v. 15c):** and drove out us
   d) **Their status Godward (v. 15d):** and please not God
   e) **Their status manward (v. 15e):** and are contrary to all men
   f) **Their opposition to evangelization of the Gentiles (v. 16a):** forbidding us to speak to the Gentiles that they may be saved
   g) **Their accumulating guilt (v. 16b):** to fill up their sins always
   h) **Their judgment (v. 16c):** but the wrath is come upon them to the uttermost

2:13 Now the apostle picks up another theme which he had touched on in 1:5a—the Thessalonians' response to the preaching of the gospel. In the Authorized Version, the word "receive" is used twice but in the original it is two different words. What Paul is saying is that when they received the message, i.e., *heard* it, they did not receive, i.e., *accept* it as the word of men but as the Word of God. The ASV brings this out clearly: "And for this cause we also thank God without ceasing, that, when ye received from us the word of the message, even the word of God, ye accepted it not as the word of men, but, as it is in truth, the word of God, which also worketh in you that believe." Paul is deeply thankful for their reception and acceptance of the message. This is another example of his selflessness. Most of us want others to believe what we say simply because *we* say it. But man's word forms a shaky foundation for faith. Only God can be fully trusted, and it is only when His Word is trusted that results are produced in hearts and lives. This is what happened to the Thessalonians—the Word was working effectively in their lives because they believed.

"His Word—the Bible—is inspired, or God-breathed, in all its books and parts as originally written. It is our only authority in all things, for all circumstances, and all times. There is needed a generation who shall tremble at the Word of God. It is life's chart; our guidance, our light, our moral safeguard. Thank God for the Sacred Volume" (Walter Scott).

2:14 What results had the Bible produced in the lives of these believers? Not only had they been saved; they were enabled to stand firm in the face of severe persecution. This was good evidence of the reality of their conversion. By their steadfast endurance, they became imitators of the Christian churches in Judea. The only difference was that the Thessalonians suffered at the hands of their Gentile countrymen, whereas the believers in Judea were persecuted by the Jews.

2:15 At this mention of the Jews, Paul launches into an indictment of them as arch-opponents of the gospel. And who should know better than he? At one time he had been a ringleader of those Jews who attempted to liquidate the Christian faith. Then after his conversion he himself felt the sharp edge of the sword of their persecution.

The crowning sin of the Jews was the killing of the Lord Jesus, for while the actual crucifixion was carried out by the Romans, it was the Jews who stirred them up to do it. This came as a climax to centuries of persecution of God's prophets sent to the nation of Israel (Matt. 21:33-39).

In the Christian era, they had already driven out Paul and other apostles, thinking mistakenly that they were pleasing God. The fact, of course, was that they were displeasing Him and making themselves obnoxious to all men.

2:16 Not content to reject the gospel themselves, they were determined to prevent Paul and his associates from preaching the message to the Gentiles. Nothing infuriated them more than to hear that Gentiles could be saved in the same way as Jews.

In their opposition to the will of God, they were carrying on where their fathers had left off "to fill up their sins always." It was as if they were determined to keep the cup of their guilt full at all times.

But their doom is pronounced, for "the wrath is come upon them to the uttermost." Paul does not specify what he means by this wrath. Perhaps it is a general statement of impending judgment as a result of a full measure of guilt. We do know that within 20 years (A.D. 70) Jerusalem was destroyed and the surviving Jews were scattered throughout the earth.

From passages such as this, some men have suggested that Paul was anti-semitic and that the New Testament is an anti-semitic book. The truth is that Paul had a deep love for his kinsmen, the Jews, and was even willing to be cut off from Christ if it could have meant their salvation (Rom. 9:1-3). Though his ministry was primarily to the Gentiles, he never lost his burden for the evangelization of the Jews; at times this burden almost seems to have taken precedence over his primary mission.

What the apostle says here about the Jewish people is historical fact and not personal invective. And we must remember that God moved him to write what he did.

Anti-semitism is unchristian and cannot be justified under any circumstances. But it is not anti-semitic to say that the Jewish people are charged by God with the death of His Son (Acts 2:23), just as the Gentiles also are held responsible for their part (1 Cor. 2:8).

VII. EXPLANATION OF PAUL'S FAILURE TO RETURN TO THESSALONICA (2:17-20)
   A. **Duration of his absence (v. 17a):** But we, brethren, being bereaved of you for a short season
   B. **Character of his absence (v. 17b):** in presence not in heart

C. His heightened desire (v. 17c): endeavored the more exceedingly to see your face with great desire

D. His two attempts to return (v. 18a): because we would fain have come unto you, I Paul once and again

E. The opposition of Satan (v. 18b): and Satan hindered us

F. Paul's high regard for the saints (vv. 19,20)

    1. What? (v. 19a): For what is our hope, or joy, or crown of glorying

    2. Who? (v. 19b): Are not even ye

    3. Where? (v. 19c): before our Lord Jesus

    4. When? (v. 19d): at his coming

    5. Why? (v. 20): For ye are our glory and our joy

2:17 In the next four verses, the apostle explains his failure to return to Thessalonica. Perhaps his carping critics accused him of cowardice in not going back because of the opposition he had encountered there.

Paul first makes it clear that the separation was only physical. The expression "being bereaved of you" means that they were orphaned by the departure of their spiritual father. However, his affectionate interest in them had never waned. Notice the words that express the intensity of his love: "endeavored . . . more exceedingly . . . great desire."

2:18 Twice he had tried to go back to Thessalonica, but twice Satan had hindered. The exact nature of Satan's opposition is not known.

Neither do we know how Paul could be sure it was the devil who hindered him and not the Lord. In Acts 16:6 we read that Paul and his party were forbidden by the Holy Spirit to preach the word in Asia. In the next verse, they tried to go to Bithynia but the Spirit would not permit them to go. How can we know when it is the Spirit and when it is the devil who is hindering? Perhaps one way is this: when we know that we are in the will of God, any hindrances that arise are not the Spirit's work but the devil's. Also Satan can be expected to hinder whenever God is blessing. But God always overrules Satan's opposition. In this particular case, Paul's inability to go to Thessalonica resulted in this letter's being written. The letter, in turn, has resulted in glory to God and blessing to us.

2:19 Why was the apostle so interested in going back to the Thessalonian believers? Because they were his children in the Lord. He had pointed them to Christ and felt responsible for their spiritual growth. He knew that he would have to give an account of them in a coming day. They were his hope of reward at the judgment seat of Christ. He wanted to be able to joy in them. They would be his crown of glory before the Lord Jesus at His coming.

It seems obvious from this verse that Paul expected to recognize the Thessalonians in heaven. And it follows that we too will know our loved ones in heaven.

In verse 19 Paul speaks of his children in the faith as being his crown. Elsewhere in the New Testament we read of other crowns: the crown of righteousness (2 Tim. 4:8); the crown of life (Jas. 1:12; Rev. 2:10); the crown of glory (1 Pet. 5:4)—all of them incorruptible (1 Cor. 9:25).

2:20 The saints were his "pride and joy." He had invested in human personality and his reward was spiritual sons and daughters who would worship the Lamb of God for all eternity.

THE COMING OF THE LORD

In verse 19, we have the first use of the word "coming" in this epistle with regard to the Lord's return. Because this is the major theme of this epistle, we are going to pause here and give a short explanation of what we believe to be the Scriptural teaching on the subject.

There are three principal Greek words used in the New

Testament with reference to Christ's return:

> parousia (pa-roo-SEE-ah) presence
> apokalupsis (apok-AL-oop-sis) unveiling, revelation
> epiphaneia (epi-FAHN-ee-ah) manifestation

The word most commonly used is *parousia*. It means a presence or a coming alongside. Vine says it denotes both an arrival and a consequent presence. In other words, when we think of the coming of the Lord, we should think of it not only as a momentary event but as a period of time.

Even in the English language, the word coming is used in this way. For instance, "Christ's coming to Galilee brought healing to multitudes." Here we do not mean the day He arrived in Galilee but the whole period of time He spent in that area.

So when we think of Christ's coming, we should think of a period of time rather than an isolated event.

Now if we take all the occurrences of *parousia* in the New Testament, we will find that they describe a period of time with:

1. A beginning
2. A course
3. A manifestation
4. A climax

1. The *beginning* of the *parousia* is the rapture. It is described in the following passages (the word which translates parousia is italicized in each case):

> "For as in Adam all die, so also in Christ shall all be made alive. But each in his own order: Christ the firstfruits; then they that are Christ's, at his *coming*" (1 Cor. 15:22,23).
> "But we would not have you ignorant, brethren, concerning them that fall asleep; that ye sorrow not, even as the rest, who have no hope. For if we believe

33

that Jesus died and rose again, even so them also that are fallen asleep in Jesus will God bring with him. For this we say unto you by the word of the Lord, that we that are alive, that are left unto the *coming* of the Lord, shall in no wise precede them that are fallen asleep. For the Lord himself shall descend from heaven, with a shout, with the voice of the archangel, and with the trump of God: and the dead in Christ shall rise first; then we that are alive, that are left, shall together with them be caught up in the clouds, to meet the Lord in the air: and so shall we ever be with the Lord. Wherefore comfort one another with these words'' (1 Thess. 4:13-18).

"Now we beseech you, brethren, touching the *coming* of our Lord Jesus Christ, and our gathering together unto him'' (2 Thess. 2:1).

"Be patient therefore, brethren, until the *coming* of the Lord. Behold, the husbandman waiteth for the precious fruit of the earth, being patient over it, until it receive the early and latter rain. Be ye also patient; establish your hearts: for the *coming* of the Lord is at hand'' (Jas. 5:7,8).

"And now, my little children, abide in him; that, if he shall be manifested, we may have boldness, and not be ashamed before him at his *coming*'' (1 John 2:28).

2. The *course* of the *parousia* includes the judgment seat of Christ when rewards will be given to believers for faithful service.

"For what is our hope, or joy, or crown of glorying? Are not even ye, before our Lord Jesus at his *coming?*'' (1 Thess. 2:19).

"And the God of peace himself sanctify you wholly; and may your spirit and soul and body be preserved entire, without blame at the *coming* of our Lord Jesus Christ'' (1 Thess. 5:23).

Another event which probably should be included in the *course* of the *parousia* is the marriage supper of the Lamb. From its location in the book of Revelation, we know that it will take place prior to Christ's glorious reign. We include it here even if the word "coming" is not used in connection with it.

"And I heard as it were the voice of a great multitude, and as the voice of many waters, and as the voice of mighty thunders, saying, Hallelujah: for the Lord our God, the Almighty, reigneth. Let us rejoice and be exceeding glad, and let us give the glory unto him: for the marriage of the Lamb is come, and his wife hath made herself ready. And it was given unto her that she should array herself in fine linen, bright and pure: for the fine linen is the righteous acts of the saints. And he saith unto me, Write, Blessed are they that are bidden to the marriage supper of the Lamb. And he saith unto me, These are true words of God" (Rev. 19:6-9).

3. The *manifestation* of Christ's coming is His return to earth in power and great glory to reign as King of kings and Lord of lords. The rapture will not be seen by the world; it takes place in a split second. But every eye will see Christ when He comes to reign. Therefore it is called the manifestation of His *parousia*. This is the third phase of His coming.

"And as he sat on the mount of Olives, the disciples came unto him privately, saying, Tell us, when shall these things be? and what shall be the sign of thy *coming,* and of the end of the world?" (Matt. 24:3).

"For as the lightning cometh forth from the east, and is seen even unto the west; so shall be the *coming* of the Son of man" (Matt. 24:27).

"And as were the days of Noah, so shall be the *coming* of the Son of man" (Matt. 24:37).

"And they knew not until the flood came, and took them all away; so shall be the *coming* of the Son of man" (Matt. 24:39).

"To the end he may establish your hearts unblameable in holiness before our God and Father, at the *coming* of our Lord Jesus with all his saints" (1 Thess. 3:13).

"And then shall be revealed the lawless one, whom the Lord Jesus shall slay with the breath of his mouth, and bring to nought by the manifestation of his *coming*" (2 Thess. 2:8).

"For we did not follow cunningly devised fables, when we made known unto you the power and *coming* of our Lord Jesus Christ, but we were eyewitnesses of his majesty" (2 Pet. 1:16). (Here Peter is speaking about the manifestation of Christ's *parousia* as it was pre-pictured on the Mount of Transfiguration.)

4. Finally we have the *climax* of the *parousia*. It is referred to in the following verse:

"And saying, Where is the promise of his *coming?* for, from the day that the fathers fell asleep, all things continue as they were from the beginning of the creation" (2 Pet. 3:4).

In this chapter we read of scoffers who will arise in the last days, denying the probability of Christ's return. What aspect of the *parousia* do they mean?

Are they referring to the rapture? No. They probably know nothing about the rapture. Are they referring to Christ's coming to reign? No. It is apparent that they are not. The entire context indicates that what they are ridiculing is the final punishment of all evildoers by the Lord. They mean a last climactic judgment of God on the earth or what they call "the end of the world." Their argument is that they have nothing to worry about. God hasn't intervened in history and He won't intervene in the future. So they feel free to continue in their evil words and deeds.

Peter answers their scoffing by pointing forward to the time, *after the thousand-year reign of Christ,* when the heavens and the earth as we now know them will be utterly destroyed. This climax of Christ's *parousia* is after the millennium and at the inauguration of the eternal state.

In addition to *parousia,* the other two words used in the original language of the New Testament to describe the coming of the Lord are *apokalupsis* and *epiphaneia.*

Apokalupsis means an unveiling or a revelation. Bible students are divided as to whether it always refers to the third phase of Christ's coming—His coming to the earth in power and glory—or whether it might also refer to the rapture when He will be revealed to the church.

In the following verses it could refer either to the rapture or the coming to reign.

"So that ye come behind in no gift; waiting for the *revelation* of our Lord Jesus Christ" (1 Cor. 1:7).

"That the proof of your faith, being more precious than gold that perisheth though it is proved by fire, may be found unto praise and glory and honor at the *revelation* of Jesus Christ" (1 Pet. 1:7).

"Wherefore girding up the loins of your mind, be sober and set your hope perfectly on the grace that is to be brought unto you at the *revelation* of Jesus Christ" (1 Pet. 1:13).

"But insomuch as ye are partakers of Christ's sufferings, rejoice; that at the *revelation* of his glory also ye may rejoice with exceeding joy" (1 Pet. 4:13).

In its other occurrence it seems to refer quite clearly to Christ's coming to reign.

"And to you that are afflicted rest with us, at the *revelation* of the Lord Jesus Christ from heaven with the angels of his power in flaming fire'' (2 Thess. 1:7).

Epiphaneia means a manifestation or an appearing. Again some think it can refer both to Christ's appearing for His saints and to His appearing with His saints; others say it refers only to the latter. The word is found in the following passages:

"And then shall be revealed the lawless one, whom the Lord Jesus shall slay with the breath of his mouth, and bring to nought by the *manifestation* of his coming'' (2 Thess. 2:8).

"That thou keep the commandment, without spot, without reproach, until the *appearing* of our Lord Jesus Christ'' (1 Tim. 6:14).

"I charge thee in the sight of God, and of Christ Jesus, who shall judge the living and the dead, and by his *appearing* and his kingdom'' (2 Tim. 4:1).

"Henceforth there is laid up for me the crown of righteousness, which the Lord, the righteous judge, shall give to me at that day; and not to me only, but also to all them that have loved his *appearing*'' (2 Tim. 4:8).

"Looking for the blessed hope and *appearing* of the glory of the great God and our Saviour Jesus Christ'' (Tit. 2:13).

The first and third verses clearly describe the appearing of Christ to the world. The others are not so clear; they could conceivably refer to the rapture also. The one thing that is clear is that both the rapture and Christ's coming to reign are held before the believer as events for which he waits with eagerness. At the time of the rapture, he will see the Savior and will receive his glorified body. When Christ returns to earth, the believer will appear with Him in glory (Col. 3:4). It is at this time also that the believer's rewards will be manifested. These rewards are given out previously

38

at the judgment seat of Christ, but they are seen by all when Christ comes to reign. What are the rewards? In Luke 19:17-19 there is a hint that they have to do with local rule in the millennium. One person is made ruler over ten cities, another over five.

By studying the various references to the Lord's coming, we have seen that it refers to a period of time rather than to a single event, and that this period of time has various phases or stages. There is a beginning, a course, a manifestation, and a climax. It begins with the rapture, includes the judgment seat of Christ, will be visibly displayed when Christ returns to earth, and will end when the heavens and earth as we now know them are destroyed by fire.

3

VIII. **THE MISSION OF TIMOTHY TO THESSA-LONICA (3:1-10)**
  A. **The intolerable burden which prompted it (v. 1a):** Wherefore when we could no longer forbear
  B. **Paul's decision to remain at Athens (v. 1b):** we thought it good to be left behind at Athens alone
  C. **Timothy sent to Thessalonica (vv. 2-10)**
    1. **His qualifications (v. 2a):** and sent Timothy, our brother and God's minister in the gospel of Christ
    2. **His ministry to the saints (vv. 2-4)**
      a) **Establishment (v. 2):** to establish you
      b) **Encouragement (vv. 2-4):** and to comfort you concerning your faith
        (1) **Afflictions should not discourage (v. 3a):** that no man be moved by these afflictions

39

- **(2) Afflictions are to be expected (v. 3b):** for yourselves know that hereunto we are appointed
- **(3) Paul had predicted afflictions (v. 4a):** For verily, when we were with you, we told you beforehand that we are to suffer affliction
- **(4) The prediction was fulfilled (v. 4b):** even as it came to pass, and ye know
3. Timothy's ministry for Paul (v. 5)
  - **a) Unbearable suspense:** For this cause I also, when I could no longer forbear
  - **b) Nagging concern:** sent that I might know your faith
  - **c) Definite danger**
    - **(1) Satan successful:** lest by any means the tempter had tempted you
    - **(2) Labor lost:** and our labor should be in vain.
4. Timothy's return and report to Paul (v. 6)
  - **a) Welcome return:** But when Timothy came even now unto us from you
  - **b) Good news:** and brought us glad tidings
    - **(1) Spiritual vigor:** of your faith and love
    - **(2) Happy memories:** and that ye have good remembrance of us always
    - **(3) Mutual longing:** longing to see us, even as we also to see you
5. Paul's relief and rejoicing (vv. 7-10)
  - **a) His great relief (v. 7a):** for this cause, brethren, we were comforted over you
  - **b) His trying circumstances (v. 7b):** in all our distress and affliction
  - **c) His specific encouragement (v. 7c):** through your faith
  - **d) His truest joy (v. 8):** for now we live, if ye stand fast in the Lord
  - **e) His overflowing thanks (v. 9):** For what

thanksgiving can we render again unto God
for you, for all the joy wherewith we joy
for your sakes before our God

f) **His earnest intercession (v. 10)**
   (1) **Its frequency:** night and day praying
   (2) **Its intensity:** exceedingly
   (3) **Its first request—reunion:** that we
       may see your face
   (4) **Its second request—completion:** and
       may perfect that which is lacking in
       your faith

The words "your faith" occur five times in this chapter
(vv. 2,5,6,7,10) and are a key to understanding the passage.
The Thessalonians were passing through severe persecution, and Paul was anxious to know how their faith was
standing up to the test. Thus the chapter is a lesson on the
importance of follow-up work. It is not enough to lead
sinners to the Savior. They must be helped to grow in grace
and in the knowledge of the Lord.

3:1 In this chapter, we continue to hear the heartbeat of
the Apostle Paul, as he expresses his undying interest in the
saints at Thessalonica. While he was at Athens, he de-
veloped an intolerable craving to know how his converts
were getting on. Satan had hindered his personal return.
Finally he could not stand inaction any longer; it was decided to send Timothy to the Thessalonians while he remained in Athens alone. The "we" is editorial.

There is a certain sadness to think of him alone at Athens.
The sights of a great city held no attraction for him; he was
burdened with the care of the churches.

3:2 Notice the degrees after Timothy's name: "our
brother and God's minister in the gospel of Christ." The
word "minister" here and elsewhere in the New Testament
simply means "servant." The idea of a separate class
known as clergymen originated in later years.

What a privilege it was for Timothy to serve his apprenticeship under the beloved brother Paul! Now that he has proved himself, he is sent on a mission to Thessalonica alone.

The purpose of the trip was to establish the saints and to comfort them concerning their faith. They had been suffering persecution because of their confession of Christ. This was a critical time for the young converts; Satan was probably dropping subtle suggestions that maybe they were wrong after all in becoming Christians.

It would be interesting to hear Timothy as he taught them to expect opposition, to bear it bravely, and to rejoice in it.

When it says that Paul sent Timothy to *comfort* them, it is not so much the thought of consolation as encouragement. They did not need sympathy in sorrow as much as they needed encouragement not to buckle under the pressure of opposition.

3:3 In the heat of persecution, it would be easy for the Thessalonians to think it strange that they should suffer so severely, and to wonder if God was displeased with them. Timothy reminded them that it wasn't strange at all, that this is normal for Christians, and that they shouldn't be shaken or lose heart.

3:4 Paul reminds them that even when he was in Thessalonica, he used to tell them that Christians are appointed to afflictions. His prediction came true in their own lives; how well they knew it!

Trials form a necessary discipline in our lives:

1. They prove the reality of our faith, and weed out those who are mere professors (1 Pet. 1:7).
2. They enable us to comfort and encourage others who are going through trials (2 Cor. 1:4).
3. They develop certain graces, such as patience, in our character (Rom. 5:3).

4. They make us more zealous in spreading the gospel (Acts 4:29; 5:27-29; 8:3,4).
5. They help to remove the dross from our lives (Job 23:10).

Can you think of any other benefits that grow out of persecution?

3:5 The apostle repeats the substance of verses 1 and 2: when further delay proved unendurable for him, he sent Timothy to find out how the Christians there were weathering the storm. His great anxiety was that the devil might have tricked them into giving up their aggressive Christian testimony in exchange for relaxation of the persecution. It is the ever-present temptation to swap loyalty to Christ for personal comfort, to by-pass the cross in pursuit of a crown. Who of us does not have to pray, "Forgive me, O Lord, for so often finding ways of avoiding the pain and sacrifice of discipleship. Strengthen me this day to walk with Thee no matter what the cost may be" (Daily Notes of the Scripture Union).

If Satan had induced the saints to recant, then Paul felt his labor there would have been for nothing.

3:6 Timothy came back to Corinth from the Thessalonians with a good report. First of all, he reassured Paul concerning their "faith and love." They were not only standing true to the teachings of the Christian faith, but they were also manifesting the distinctive virtue of love. This is ever the test of reality—not just an orthodox acceptance of the Christian creed, but "faith working through love" (Gal. 5:6). Not just your "faith in the Lord Jesus" but also your "love . . . toward all the saints" (Eph. 1:15).

Was it significant that Timothy mentioned their faith and love, but omitted any reference to their hope? Had the devil shaken their confidence in the return of Christ? That may be so. As William Lincoln said, "The devil hates that doctrine because he knows the power of it in our lives." If their hope was defective, Paul certainly seeks to repair it in this epistle of hope.

Timothy also reported that the Thessalonians had kind memories of Paul and his friends, and that they were as anxious for a reunion as the apostle, Silas, and Timothy were.

3:7 This news was like cold water to Paul's thirsty soul (Prov. 25:25). In all his distress and affliction, he was greatly encouraged through their faith.

3:8 He exclaims, "For now we live, if ye stand fast in the Lord." The suspense of not knowing had been a living death to him. Now life quickly returned when he heard that all was well. What a commentary this is on the unselfish devotion of this great man of God!

3:9 Words failed to express adequately to God the thanksgiving which filled Paul's heart. His cup of joy was overflowing every time he remembered them before the Lord.

3:10 Paul's prayer life was habitual, not spasmodic: "night and day." It was intensely fervent: "praying exceedingly." It was specific: "that we may see your face." And it was altruistic: "and may perfect that which is lacking in your faith."

It is interesting to notice that he did not pray for their material welfare but for their spiritual good. "Soul prosperity is the best prosperity."

IX. PAUL'S SPECIFIC PRAYER (3:11-13)
   A. **For a return trip to them (v. 11):** Now may our God and Father himself, and our Lord Jesus, direct our way unto you
   B. **For greater love in them (vv. 12,13)**
      1. **Its measure (v. 12a):** and the Lord make you to increase and abound in love

    2. Its objects (v. 12b): one toward another, and toward all men

    3. Its pattern (v. 12c): even as we also do toward you

    4. Its outcome (v. 13)

      a) Blameless condition: to the end he may establish your hearts unblameable in holiness

      b) Privileged position: before our God and Father

      c) Glorious occasion: at the coming of our Lord Jesus with all his saints

3:11 The chapter closes with Paul's prayer for a return trip to them, and for the development of even greater love in them.

The request is addressed to "our God and Father himself, and our Lord Jesus." Then this plural subject is followed by a singular verb. What does this suggest to you concerning the Person of the Lord Jesus?

3:12 The Thessalonians had actually been commendable in manifesting true Christian love, but there is always room for development. And so he prays for a deeper measure: "the Lord make you to increase and abound in love." Their love should embrace their fellow believers and all men, including their enemies. Its model or pattern should be the love of the apostles: "Even as we also do toward you."

3:13 The result of love in this life is blamelessness in the next. If we love one another and all mankind, we will stand unblameable in holiness before God when Christ comes with all His saints, for love is the fulfilling of the law (Rom. 13:8; Jas. 2:8).

Someone has paraphrased the prayer as follows: "The Lord enable you more and more to spend your lives in the interests of others, in order that He may so establish you in Christian character now, that you might be vindicated from

45

every charge that might possibly be brought against you. . . .''

In chapter 2, we mentioned that the coming of Christ has several stages or phases: a beginning, a course, a manifestation, and a climax. It is the third phase that is referred to here in verse 13—the coming of our Lord Jesus with all His saints. The judgment seat of Christ will have already taken place in heaven. The awards will already have been made. But these awards will be manifested to all when the Savior returns to earth as King of kings and Lord of lords.

''Saints'' here in verse 13 probably means those believers who have been caught up to heaven at the time of the rapture (1 Thess. 4:14). Some think that it means angels, but Vincent says it refers to *the holy and glorified people of God*. He points out that angels have nothing to do with anything in this Epistle, but that glorified believers are closely connected with the subject that was troubling the Thessalonians. He adds, ''This does not exclude the attendance of angels on the Lord's coming, but when Paul speaks of such attendance, he says *with the angels of his power,* as in 2 Thessalonians 1:7.''

4

X. **THE LIFE THAT PLEASES GOD (4:1)**
   A. **The pointed appeal:** Finally then, brethren, we beseech and exhort you in the Lord Jesus
   B. **The past instruction:** that, as ye received of us
   C. **The proper behavior:** how ye ought to walk and to please God
   D. **The present performance:** even as ye do walk
   E. **The permanent challenge:** that ye abound more and more

4:1 The word "Finally" doesn't necessarily mean that Paul is about to close the letter. It often indicates a change of subject such as a shift to practical exhortations.

Three prominent words at the close of chapter 3 were holiness, love, and coming. These are three of the principal subjects of chapter 4:

1. Holiness (vv. 1-8)
2. Love (vv. 9,10)
3. Coming (vv. 13-18)

The other main theme is industriousness (vv. 11,12).

The chapter opens with a plea to walk in holiness and thus to please God, and closes with the translation of the saints. There is little doubt that Paul was thinking of Enoch when he wrote this. Notice the similarity.

1. Enoch walked with God (Gen. 5:24a)
2. Enoch pleased God (Heb. 11:5b)
3. Enoch was translated (Gen. 5:24b; Heb. 11:5a)

The apostle commends the believers for their practical holiness, but urges them to advance to new levels of accomplishment. Holiness is a process, not an achievement.

XI. **THE SANCTIFICATION THAT FULFILLS HIS WILL (4:2-8)**
   A. **Paul's instructions (v. 2a):** For ye know what charge we gave you
   B. **Christ's authority (v. 2b):** through the Lord Jesus
   C. **God's will (vv. 3-8):** For this is the will of God, even your sanctification, that ye abstain from fornication
      1. **Practice self-control (vv. 4,5):** that each one of you know how to possess himself of his own vessel

a) **The right way (v. 4b):** in sanctification and honor
b) **The wrong way (v. 5):** not in the passion of lust even as the Gentiles who know not God
2. **Respect the rights of others (v. 6a):** that no man transgress, and wrong his brother in the matter
3. **Fear the Divine Avenger (v. 6b):** because the Lord is an avenger in all these things
4. **Remember the apostle's words (v. 6c):** as also we forewarned you and testified
5. **Realize the purpose of God's call (v. 7):** For God called us not for uncleanness, but in sanctification
6. **Recognize the peril of disobedience (v. 8):** Therefore he that rejecteth, rejecteth not man, but God, who giveth his Holy Spirit unto you

4:2 While he was with them, Paul repeatedly charged them, with the authority of the Lord Jesus, that they should please God by lives of practical holiness.

4:3 God's will for His people is their sanctification. To sanctify means to set apart for divine use. In one sense, all believers have been set apart from the world to the service of the Lord; this is known as positional sanctification, and it is perfect and complete (1 Cor. 1:2; Heb. 10:10). However, in another sense, believers should sanctify themselves, that is, they should separate themselves from all forms of sin; this is known as practical or progressive sanctification. It is a process that will continue until the believer's death or the Lord's return. It is this latter use of the word that is found in verse 3.

The specific sin against which Paul warns is fornication. This is unlawful sexual intercourse, and in this section is probably the same as adultery. It is one of the principal sins of the heathen world. The admonition, ''that ye abstain from fornication,'' is needed today as it was needed in the first century of the church.

4:4 The Christian program is for every one to possess his vessel in sanctification and honor. The word ''vessel'' in this verse may mean a wife or it may mean the man's own body. It is used of a wife in 1 Peter 3:7 and of the body in 2 Corinthians 4:7.

The RSV understands it to mean a wife: ''that each one of you know how to take a wife for himself in holiness and honor.''

The NEB adopts the view that the body is meant: ''every one of you must learn to gain mastery over his body, to hallow and honor it.''

If we allow the context to decide, then ''vessel'' means the man's wife. The teaching is that each man should treat his wife honorably and decently, never stooping to any form of marital unfaithfulness. The expression ''his own wife'' reinforces monogamy as God's will for mankind (see also 1 Cor. 7:2).

4:5 The Christian view of marriage is in sharp contrast to that of the ungodly. As one commentator said, ''When Jesus laid His hands on the woman in Luke 13:13, she was made straight. When pagan man touches a woman, she is made crooked.''

The Gentiles think of sex as a means of gratifying the passion of lust. To them chastity is a weakness and marriage a means of making sin religious. By their filthy conversation and their obscene writings on public walls, they glory in their shame.

4:6 Sexual immorality is a sin against God's Holy Spirit (1 Cor. 6:19); it is a sin against one's own body (1 Cor. 6:18); but it is also a sin against other persons. So Paul adds: ''. . . that no man transgress and wrong his brother in the matter. . . .'' In other words, a Christian must not go beyond the bounds of marriage and defraud a brother by

49

stealing the affections of the brother's wife. Though these offenses are not generally punished in criminal courts today, God is the avenger of all such. Sexual sins bring on a terrible harvest of physical and mental disorders in this life, but these are nothing compared to their eternal consequences, if they are unconfessed and unforgiven. Paul had previously warned the Thessalonians of this.

One of Britain's greatest writers of the nineteenth century fell into sexual sin and ended in prison and disgrace. He wrote: "The gods have given me almost everything. But I let myself be lured into long spells of senseless and sensual ease. . . . Tired of being on the heights I deliberately went to the depths in search for new sensation. . . . *I grew careless of the lives of others*. I took pleasure where it pleased me and passed on. I forgot that every little action of the common day makes or unmakes character, and that therefore what one has done in the secret chamber, one has some day to cry aloud from the housetop. I ceased to be lord over myself. I was no longer the captain of my soul, and did not know it. I allowed pleasure to dominate me. I ended in horrible disgrace."

He grew careless of the lives of others, or, as Paul would say, he transgressed and wronged his brother in the matter.

4:7 God has not called us on the basis of moral uncleanness but in connection with lives of holiness and purity. He has called us from a cesspool of degradation, and has begun in us a lifelong process designed to make us more and more like Himself.

4:8 Anyone who despises this instruction isn't simply rejecting the teaching of a man, such as Paul; he is defying, disregarding, flouting, and rejecting God Himself—Who has given us His *Holy* Spirit. The word *Holy* is emphatic here. How can one who is indwelt by the *Holy* Spirit indulge in sexual sin?

Notice that all members of the Trinity are mentioned in this paragraph.

The Father (v. 3)
The Son (v. 2)
The Holy Spirit (v. 8)

Wonderful thought! All three Persons in the Godhead are interested and involved in the sanctification of the believer.

XII. THE LOVE THAT THINKS OF OTHERS (4:9,10)

A. **An obvious reminder (v. 9a):** But concerning love of the brethren ye have no need that one write unto you
B. **A divine instinct (v. 9b):** for ye yourselves are taught of God to love one another
C. **A commendable practice (v. 10a):** for indeed ye do it toward all the brethren that are in all Macedonia
D. **A continuing duty (v. 10b):** But we exhort you, brethren, that ye abound more and more

Someone has pointed out that the subject changes now from lust (vv. 1-8) to love (vv. 9-12), and the exhortation changes from abstain to abound.

4:9 Not only is the believer to have a controlled body; he should also have a heart of love for his brothers in the Lord. Love is the keyword of Christianity as sin is of heathenism.

There was no need to write to the Thessalonians about this virtue. God taught them to love their brothers, both by divine instinct (1 John 2:20,27) and by the instruction of Christian teachers.

The believers at Thessalonica distinguished themselves by loving all the Christians in all of Macedonia. By commending them for it, Paul memorialized them for ever.

4:10 As has been mentioned, brotherly kindness is not an achievement; it is something that must be practiced continually, and so Paul exhorts the believers to abound more and more in this grace.

Why is love of the brethren so important? Because where there is love, there is unity; and where there is unity, there is the Lord's blessing (Psa. 133:1,3).

XIII. THE LIFE THAT SPEAKS TO OUTSIDERS (4:11,12)

A. A worthy ambition (v. 11a): and that ye study to be quiet

B. A full-time occupation (v. 11b): and to do your own business

C. A steady diligence (v. 11c): and to work with your hands, even as we charged you

D. An exemplary life (v. 12a): that ye may walk becomingly toward them that are without

E. An honorable independence (v. 12b): and may have need of nothing

4:11 Paul encouraged the saints to study to do three things. Here the word "study" means "be ambitious" or "make it one's aim." It is also found in Romans 15:20 and 2 Corinthians 5:9. In today's language the three commands in this verse would be:

1. Don't seek after the limelight. Be content to be "little and unknown, loved and prized by Christ alone."
2. Mind your own business instead of butting into other people's affairs.
3. Be self-supporting. Don't be a drone or a parasite, sponging off others.

4:12 The fact that we are Christians and that we look for Christ's coming does not relieve us of the practical responsibilities of life. We should remember that the world is watching us. Men judge our Savior by us. We should walk honestly (becomingly) toward unbelievers and be independent of them financially.

XIV. THE HOPE THAT COMFORTS BELIEVERS (4:13-18)

A. The outlook for saints who have died (vv. 13,14)

1. **No need for continued ignorance (v. 13a):** But we would not have you ignorant, brethren, concerning them that fall asleep

2. **No need for hopeless sorrow (v. 13b):** that ye sorrow not, even as the rest, who have no hope

3. **The historical pledge (v. 14a):** For if we believe that Jesus died and rose again

4. **The prophetical fulfillment (v. 14b)**
   a) **The risen saints:** even so them also that are fallen asleep in Jesus
   b) **The righteous God:** will God
   c) **The returning King:** bring with him

5. **A general assurance concerning the dead in Christ (v. 15)**
   a) **Divine revelation:** For this we say unto you by the word of the Lord
   b) **Comforting declaration:** that we that are alive, that are left unto the coming of the Lord, shall in no wise precede them that are fallen asleep

B. The order of events at His coming (vv. 16,17)

1. **Our beloved Lord (v. 16a):** For the Lord himself

2. **His glorious descent (v. 16b):** shall descend from heaven

3. **Three resounding calls (v. 16c):** with a shout, with the voice of the archangel, and with the trump of God

4. **Dead saints raised (v. 16d):** and the dead in Christ shall rise first

5. **A simultaneous rapture (v. 17a):** then we that are alive, that are left, shall together with them be caught up in the clouds

6. At last—face to face (v. 17b): to meet the Lord in the air

7. Then eternal communion (v. 17c): and so shall we ever be with the Lord

C. His coming a basis for mutual encouragement (v. 18): Wherefore comfort one another with these words

4:13 Believers in the Old Testament had very imperfect and incomplete knowledge of what happens to a person at the time of death. To them sheol was an all-purpose word used to describe the disembodied state, both of believers and unbelievers.

They believed that everyone would die eventually, that there would be one general resurrection at the end of the world, and then a final judgment. Martha reflected these sketchy views when she said, "I know that he (Lazarus) shall rise again in the resurrection at the last day" (John 11:24).

The Lord Jesus brought life and immortality to light by the gospel (2 Tim. 1:10). Today we know that the believer departs to be with Christ at the time of death (2 Cor. 5:8; Phil. 1:21,23). The unbeliever is said to be in hades (Luke 16:22,23, RV). We know that not all believers will die, but that all will be changed (1 Cor. 15:51). We know that there will be more than one resurrection. At the rapture, only believers will be raised (1 Cor. 15:23; 1 Thess. 4:16); the wicked dead will be raised at the end of the thousand-year reign of Christ (Rev. 20:5).

When the Apostle Paul first went to Thessalonica, he taught the Christians about Christ's coming to reign and the events that would follow. But in the meantime, problems had arisen regarding those saints who had died. Would their bodies remain in the graves until the last day? Would they be excluded from participation in Christ's coming and in His glorious kingdom? To answer their questions and allay their fears, Paul now describes the order of events at the time of Christ's coming for His people.

54

The formula, "we would not have you ignorant, brethren," is used to alert readers to an important announcement.

Here the announcement concerns those who have fallen asleep, that is, those believers who have died. Sleep is used to describe the bodies of departed Christians, never their spirits or souls. Sleep is an appropriate simile of death, because in death a person seems to be sleeping. Even our word cemetery comes from a Greek word meaning rest house or sleeping place. And sleep is a familiar simile, because every night we act out this symbol of death, and every morning is like a resurrection.

The Bible does not teach that the soul sleeps at the time of death. The rich man and Lazarus were both conscious in death (Luke 16:19-31). When the believer dies, he is "at home with the Lord" (2 Cor. 5:8). To die is to "be with Christ," a position which Paul speaks of as "gain" and as being "far better" (Phil. 1:21,23). This would scarcely be true if the soul were sleeping.

Neither does the Bible teach annihilation. There is no cessation of being in death. The believer enjoys eternal life (Mark 10:30). The unbeliever suffers eternal punishment (Mark 9:48; Rev. 14:11).

With regard to those saints who have died, the apostle says that there is no need for hopeless sorrow. He does not rule out sorrow; Jesus wept at the grave of Lazarus, though He knew He would raise him in a few minutes (John 11:35-44). But he rules out the despairing grief of those who have no hope of heaven, of reunion, of anything but judgment.

The expression "the rest who have no hope" invariably reminds me of a funeral I attended where the stricken relatives clustered around the casket of an unsaved relative and wailed inconsolably, "Oh, Marie, my God, my God, Marie." It was an unforgettable scene of unrelieved hopelessness.

4:14 The basis of the believer's hope is the resurrection of Christ. Just as surely as we believe that He died and rose again, so we believe that those who have fallen asleep in

Jesus will be raised and will participate in His coming. "For as in Adam all die, so also in Christ shall all be made alive" (1 Cor. 15:22). His resurrection is the pledge and proof of ours.

Notice the expression "fallen asleep in Jesus." Some translations say "fallen asleep through Jesus." This robs death of its terror—to know that it is merely the Lover of our souls giving sleep to the bodies of His beloved ones.

Our positive assurance concerning those who have died in Christ is that God will bring them with Him. This may be understood in two ways:

1. It may mean that at the time of the rapture, God will raise the bodies of believers and bring them back to heaven with the Lord Jesus.
2. Or it may mean that when Christ comes back to the earth to reign, God will bring back with Christ those who have died in faith. In other words, the apostle is saying, "Don't worry that those who have died will miss out in the glory of the coming kingdom. God will bring them back with Jesus when the latter returns in power and great glory." (This is the generally preferred meaning.)

But how can this be? Their bodies are now lying in the grave. How can they come back with Jesus? The answer is given in verses 15-17. Before Christ comes to set up His kingdom, He will return to take His own people home to be with Him in heaven. Then at a later date, He will come back with them.

4:15 How did Paul know this? His answer is, "this we say unto you by the word of the Lord." Which simply means that he received this as a direct revelation from the Lord. We are not told how he received it—whether by a vision, by an audible voice, or by the inward impression of the Holy Spirit. But it is definitely a truth hitherto unknown to the sons of men.

Then he goes on to explain that when Christ returns, the living saints will not have any precedence or advantage over sleeping saints. (The word "prevent" in the AV is an old-fashioned word for "precede.")

In this verse Paul speaks of himself as one who would be alive at Christ's return (see also 1 Cor. 15:51,52). However, in 2 Corinthians 4:14 and 5:1, he speaks of the possibility of his being among those who will be raised. The obvious conclusion is that we should look for the Lord to come at any moment, yet realize that we may be called to reach heaven by way of death.

4:16 The exact order of events at Christ's coming for His saints is now given. "The Lord Himself shall descend from heaven." He will not send an angel, but will come Himself.

It will be with a shout, with the voice of the archangel, and with the trump of God. Several explanations have been offered as to the significance of these commanding sounds, and frankly it is almost impossible to speak with finality about them:

1. Some feel that the shout is the voice of the Lord Jesus Himself which raises the dead (John 5:25; 11:43,44) and changes the living. Others, like Hogg and Vine, say that the shout is in the archangel's voice.
2. The voice of Michael, the archangel, is commonly understood as an assembling command for the Old Testament saints, since the archangel is so closely associated with Israel (Dan. 12:1; Jude 9; Rev. 12:4-7). Others think its purpose is to revive Israel nationally. And still others suggest the voice of the archangel summons the angels as a military escort to accompany the Lord and His saints through enemy territory back to heaven (compare Luke 16:22).
3. The trump of God is the same as the last trump of 1 Corinthians 15:52, which has to do with the resurrection of believers at the time of the rapture. It calls the

saints to eternal blessing. It is not to be confused with the seventh trumpet of Revelation 11:15-18, which signals the final outpouring of judgment on the world during the tribulation. The last trump here is the last for the church. The seventh trumpet of Revelation is the last for the unbelieving world (though it is never specifically called the "last trumpet").

The bodies of the dead in Christ shall rise first. Whether this includes the Old Testament saints is debatable. Those who think it does point out that the archangel's voice is heard at this time, and that he is closely linked with the destinies of Israel (Dan. 12:1). Those who think that the Old Testament saints will not be raised at the rapture remind us that the phrase "in Christ" (the dead "in Christ") is never applied to believers who lived before the church age; these believers will probably be raised at the end of the tribulation (Dan. 12:2). In any case it is clear that this is not a general resurrection. Not all the dead are raised at this time, but only the dead in Christ.

4:17 Then the living will be caught up together with them in the clouds to meet the Lord in the air. The word rapture which we use to describe this first phase of the Lord's return has its origin in a Latin word meaning *caught up*. A rapture is a snatching away or a catching up. It is used of Philip in Acts 8:39, of Paul in 2 Corinthians 12:2,4, and of the man child in Revelation 12:5.

The air, of course, is Satan's sphere (Eph. 2:2), so this is a triumphal gathering in open defiance of the devil and in his stronghold.

Think of all that is included in these verses. The earth and the sea yielding up the dust of all the dead in Christ. Then the transforming miracle by which this dust is formed into glorified bodies, free forever from sickness, pain, and death. Then the space-flight to heaven. And all of this taking place in the twinkling of an eye (1 Cor. 15:52).

Men of the world have difficulty believing the account of

the creation of man in Genesis 1 and 2. If they have difficulty with creation, what will they do with the rapture when God will recreate millions of people from dust that has been buried, scattered, strewn, or swept up on the beaches of the world?

Men of the world are enthusiastic about space travel. But can their greatest exploits compare with the wonder of traveling to heaven in a split second without taking our own atmosphere with us, as the space men have to do when they go on short hops to outer space?

Someone has pointed out in connection with Christ's coming that there is a sound to hear, a sight to see, a miracle to feel, a meeting to enjoy, and a comfort to experience.

It is also good to notice the recurrence of the word *Lord* in these verses: the word of the Lord (v. 15), the coming of the Lord (v. 15), the Lord Himself (v. 16), to meet the Lord (v. 17), to be forever with the Lord (v. 17).

Forever with the Lord!! Who can tell all the joy and blessedness that are included in these words?

4:18 "Wherefore comfort one another with these words." Thoughts of the Lord's coming do not produce terror for the believer. It is a hope that thrills and cheers and comforts.

There are many indications that the rapture may be very near. We consider the following as straws in the wind.

1. The formation of the State of Israel in 1948 (Luke 21:29). The fig tree (Israel) is shooting forth, that is, is putting forth its leaves (Luke 21:29-31). For the first time in centuries, the Jews have a national existence in their own homeland. This means that the kingdom of God is near.
2. The rise of many other nations (Luke 21:29). Jesus predicted that not only the fig tree would shoot forth but all the trees as well. We have recently witnessed the decline of colonial governments and the proliferation of new nations. It is an era of new nationalism.

3. The return of Israel to the land in unbelief (Ezek. 36:24,25). Ezekiel prophesied that it would only be after their return that they would be cleansed from their sins. Israel today is largely a godless nation; only a small segment of the people are orthodox Jews.

4. The ecumenical movement (Rev. 17, 18). We understand Babylon the Great to be a vast religious, political, and commercial system made up of apostate religious bodies that profess to be Christian, perhaps a merger of apostate Catholicism and apostate Protestantism. Christendom is becoming increasingly apostate (1 Tim. 4:1; 2 Thess. 2:3) and is moving toward a world superchurch.

5. The worldwide increase in spiritism (1 Tim. 4:1-3). It is sweeping over vast areas of the earth at this moment.

6. The drastic decline of moral standards (2 Tim. 3:1-5). The daily newspapers offer plenty of evidence that this is occurring.

7. Violence and civil disobedience (2 Thess. 2:7,8). A spirit of lawlessness is abounding in the home, in national life, and even in the church.

8. People with a form of godliness but denying the power thereof (2 Tim. 3:5).

9. The rise of the anti-Christian spirit (1 John 2:18), manifested in the multiplication of false cults which profess to be Christian but deny every fundamental doctrine of the faith. They deceive by imitation (2 Tim. 3:8).

10. The tendency for nations to confederate along lines that approximate the line-up of the latter day. The European Common Market, based on what is known as the Treaty of Rome, may lead to the revival of the Roman Empire—the ten toes of iron and clay (Dan. 2:32-35).

11. Denial of the impending intervention of God in the affairs of the world by way of judgment (2 Pet. 3:3,4).

To these could be added such straws in the wind as earthquakes in many countries, the threat of worldwide famine, and the increasing hostility among nations (Matt. 24:6,7). The failure of governments to maintain law and order and to suppress terrorism creates the climate for a world dictator. The building of nuclear arsenals gives added meaning to such questions as, "Who is able to make war with him?" i.e., the beast (Rev. 13:4). Worldwide television facilities may be the means for fulfilling Scriptures describing events that will be seen simultaneously all over planet earth (Rev. 1:7).

Most of these events are foreseen as occurring before the Lord Jesus Christ returns to the earth to reign. The Bible does not say they will take place before the rapture but before His appearing in glory. If that is so, and if we see these trends developing already, then the obvious conclusion is that the rapture must be very near at hand.

5

XV. THE DAY OF THE LORD (5:1-11)

A. **A written account unneeded (v. 1):** But concerning the times and the seasons, brethren, ye have no need that aught be written unto you.

B. **Its coming in reference to unbelievers (vv. 2,3)**

1. **Unexpectedly (v. 2):** For yourselves know perfectly that the day of the Lord so cometh as a thief in the night

2. **Deceptively (v. 3a):** When they are saying, Peace and safety

3. **Suddenly (v. 3b):** then sudden

4. **Destructively (v. 3c):** destruction cometh upon them

5. Inevitably (v. 3d): as travail upon a woman with child

6. Inescapably (v. 3e): and they shall in no wise escape

C. Its coming in reference to believers (vv. 4-11)

   1. Not in darkness (v. 4a): But ye, brethren, are not in darkness

   2. Not in danger (v. 4b): that that day should overtake you as a thief

   3. Sons of light (v. 5a): for ye are all sons of light, and sons of the day

   4. Not of night (v. 5b): we are not of the night, nor of darkness

   5. While others are asleep (v. 6a): so then let us not sleep, as do the rest

   6. Our sober watch we keep (v. 6b): but let us watch and be sober

   7. Night is for drowsing (v. 7a): For they that sleep sleep in the night

   8. And for carousing (v. 7b): and they that are drunken are drunken in the night

   9. Called to sobriety (v. 8a): But let us, since we are of the day, be sober

  10. Armored with piety (v. 8b): putting on the breastplate of faith and love; and for a helmet, the hope of salvation

  11. Not the fear of condemnation (v. 9a): For God appointed us not unto wrath

  12. But the hope of full salvation (vv. 9b,10): but unto the obtaining of salvation

    a) The blessed Savior (v. 9c): through our Lord Jesus Christ

    b) The cost of our salvation (v. 10a): who died

    c) The substitutionary nature of His death (v. 10b): for us

    d) Its comprehensive character (v. 10c): that, whether we wake or sleep

> **e) Its eventual goal (v. 10d):** we should live
> together with him
> **13. Cheering exhortation (v. 11a):** Wherefore
> exhort one another
> **14. Continuing edification (v. 11b):** and build
> each other up, even as also ye do

5:1 Bible teachers often have to apologize for chapter breaks, explaining that the subject should continue without interruption. But here is a case where the chapter break is appropriate. Paul now begins a new subject. He leaves his discussion of the rapture and turns to the day of the Lord. The words translated "But" (Gr. *peri de*) indicate a new line of thought.

For true believers the rapture is a comforting hope, but what will it mean for those who are outside of Christ? It will mean the beginning of a period referred to here as *the times and the seasons*. This period is primarily Jewish in character; during this time God will resume His dealings with the nation of Israel, and the endtime events to which the Old Testament prophets pointed will occur. When the apostles asked Jesus when He would set up His kingdom, He answered that it was not for them to know the times and the seasons (Acts 1:7). It seems that the times and seasons cover the period prior to the setting up of the kingdom as well as the kingdom itself.

Paul did not feel it was necessary to write to the Thessalonians about the times and the seasons. For one thing, the saints would not be affected by them; they would be taken to heaven before these epochs began.

The times and the seasons and the day of the Lord are subjects that are found in the Old Testament. The rapture is a mystery (1 Cor. 15:51), never revealed until the time of the apostles.

5:2 The saints already knew about the day of the Lord. They knew that the exact time was unknown, but that it would come when least expected.

What does Paul mean by the day of the Lord? It is certainly not a day of 24 hours, but a period of time with certain characteristics.

In the Old Testament it was used to describe any time of judgment, desolation, and darkness (Isa. 2:12; 3:9-11; Joel 2:1,2). It was a time when God marched forth against the enemies of Israel and punished them decisively (Zeph. 3:8-12; Joel 3:14-16; Obad. 15-17; Zech. 12:8,9). But it was also any occasion on which God punished His own people for their idolatry and backsliding (Joel 1:15-20; Amos 5:18; Zeph. 1:7-18). Basically it spoke of judgment on sin, of victory for the cause of the Lord (Joel 2:31,32), and blessing for His faithful people.

In the future, the day of the Lord will cover approximately the same period as the times and the seasons. It will begin after the rapture and will include:

1. The tribulation, i.e., the time of Jacob's trouble (Dan. 9:27; Jer. 30:7; Matt. 24:4-28; 2 Thess. 2:2, ASV; Rev. 6:1—19:16).
2. The coming of Christ with His saints (Mal. 4:1-3; 2 Thess. 1:7-9).
3. The thousand-year reign of Christ on the earth (Joel 3:18, cp. v. 14; Zech. 14:8,9, cp. v.1).
4. The final destruction of the heavens and earth by fire (2 Pet. 3:7,10).

The day of the Lord is the time when Jehovah will publicly intervene in human affairs. It is characterized by judgment on the enemies of Israel and upon the apostate portion of the nation of Israel, deliverance of His people, establishment of Christ's kingdom of peace and prosperity, and glory for Himself.

The apostle reminds his readers that the day of the Lord will come as a thief in the night. It will be completely unexpected, taking men off guard. The world will be wholly unprepared.

5:3 As suggested in the outline, it will also come deceptively, suddenly, destructively, inevitably, and inescapably.

There will be an air of confidence and security in the world. Then God's judgment will suddenly begin to descend with vast destructive force. Destruction does not mean loss of being, or annihilation; it means loss of well-being or ruin as far as the purpose of one's existence is concerned. It will be as inevitable and unavoidable as the excruciating pain which seizes a woman giving birth to a child. From this judgment there will be no escape for those who are unbelievers.

5:4 It is important to notice the change in pronouns from ''they'' and ''them'' in the previous verses to ''ye, you, we, us'' in this verse.

The day of the Lord will be a time of wrath for the unsaved world. But what will it mean to us? The answer is that we are not in danger because we are not in darkness.

The day of the Lord will come as a thief in the night (v. 2). The only way it will overtake anyone is as a thief, and the only persons it will overtake will be those who are in the night, that is, the unconverted. It will not overtake believers at all, because they are not ''in darkness.''

At first reading, this verse might seem to say that the day of the Lord *will* overtake believers but *not as a thief*. But this is not so. It *will not overtake them at all* because when the thief comes to this world's night, the saints will be dwelling in eternal light.

5:5 All Christians are sons of light, and sons of the day. They are not of the night nor of darkness. It is this fact that will exempt them from the judgment that God will pour out on the world that has rejected His Son. The judgments of the day of the Lord are aimed only at those who are in moral darkness and spiritual night, at those who are alienated from God.

When it says here that Christians are sons of the day, it does not mean the day of the Lord. To be sons of the day means to be people who belong to the realm of moral uprightness. The day of the Lord is a time of judgment on those who belong to the realm of moral darkness.

5:6 The next three verses call believers to a life that is consistent with their exalted position. This means watchfulness and sobriety. We are to watch against temptation, sloth, lethargy, and distraction. Positively we should watch for the Savior's return.

Sobriety here means not only soberness in conversation and in general demeanor but temperance as far as food and drink are concerned.

5:7 In the natural realm, sleep is associated with nighttime. So in the spiritual realm careless indifference characterizes those who are sons of darkness, that is, the unconverted.

Men prefer to carry on their drunken revelry at night; they love darkness rather than light because their deeds are evil (John 3:19). Even the name "night club" links the ideas of drinking and carousing with the darkness of night.

5:8 Those who are sons of the day should walk in the light as He is in the light (1 John 1:7). This means judging and forsaking sin, and avoiding excesses of all kinds.

It also means putting on the Christian armor and keeping it on. The armor consists of the breastplate of faith and love, and the helmet of the hope of salvation. In other words, the armor is faith, love, and hope—the three cardinal elements of Christian character. It is not necessary to press the details of the breastplate and the helmet. The apostle is simply saying that sons of light should wear the protective covering of a consistent, godly life. What preserves us from the corruption that is in the world through lust? Faith, or dependence on God. Love for the Lord and for one another. The hope of Christ's return.

Unbelievers ("they")	Believers ("you")
Sleeping	Not sleeping
Drunken	Not drunken
In darkness	Not in darkness
Of the night and of darkness	Sons of light and sons of the day
Overtaken unexpectedly by the day of the Lord as a thief in the night	Not overtaken by the day of the Lord as a thief
Sudden and inescapable destruction, as travail on a pregnant woman	Not appointed to wrath but to obtain salvation

5:9 The rapture has two aspects, salvation and wrath. For the believer it means the consummation of his salvation in heaven. For the unbeliever, it means the ushering in of a time of wrath on earth.

Since we are of the day, we are not appointed to the wrath which God will pour out during the tribulation period, but rather to salvation in its fullest sense—freedom forever from the very presence of sin.

Some understand "wrath" here to refer to the punishment which unbelievers will suffer in hell. It is of course true that God has not appointed us to that, but it is gratuitous to introduce that thought here. Paul is not talking about hell but about future events on earth. The context deals with the day of the Lord—the greatest period of wrath in the history of man on earth (Matt. 24:21). We do not have an appointment with the executioner but with the Savior.

There are some who say that the tribulation is the time of Satan's wrath (Rev. 12:12), not the wrath of God. They say that the church will experience the wrath of Satan but will be delivered from the wrath of God at the Second Coming of Christ. However, the following verses speak of the wrath of God and of the Lamb, and their setting is during the tribulation period: Revelation 6:16,17; 14:9,10,19; 15:1,7; 16:1,19.

5:10 This verse emphasizes the tremendous price our Lord Jesus Christ paid to deliver us from wrath and insure our salvation. He died for us that whether awake or asleep we should live together with Him.

There are two ways of understanding the expression "awake or asleep." Some able Bible scholars understand it to mean "living or dead" at the time of the rapture. They point out that there will be two classes of believers at that time—those who have died in Christ, and those who are still living. So the thought is that whether we are among the living or the dead at the time of Christ's return, we shall live with Him. Christians who die lose nothing. The Lord explained this to Martha: "I am the resurrection and the life: he that believeth on me, though he die (i.e., a Christian who dies before the rapture), yet shall he live (he will be raised from among the dead), and whosoever liveth and believeth on me (a believer who is alive at the time of the rapture) shall never die" (John 11:25,26).

The other view, held by equally able students of the Word, is that "awake or asleep" means "watchful or worldly." In other words, Paul is saying that whether we are spiritually alert or carnally indifferent to spiritual things, we will be caught up to meet the Lord. Our eternal salvation does not depend on our spiritual keenness during the closing moments of our time on earth. If truly converted, we will live together with Him when He comes again, whether we are on the tiptoes of expectancy or in the prone position of slumber. Our spiritual condition will determine our rewards, but our salvation depends on faith in Christ alone.

Those who hold this second view point out that the word for "wake" is the same word translated "watch" in verse 6. And the word for "sleep" is used in verses 6 and 7 to mean "insensitivity to divine things, involving conformity to the world" (Vine). But it is not the same word used in 4:13,14,15 to mean death.

5:11 In view of so great salvation, in love for so great a Savior, and in the light of His soon return, we should exhort one another by teaching, encouragement, and example, and we should build each other up with the word of God and with loving care. Because we will live together with Him then, we should live together with one another cooperatively now.

XVI. VARIED EXHORTATIONS TO THE SAINTS (5:12-22)

A. Responsibility of Christians to their spiritual leaders (vv. 12,13)

1. **Recognition (v. 12):** But we beseech you, brethren, to know them
   a) **Workers:** that labor among you
   b) **Leaders:** and are over you in the Lord
   c) **Instructors:** and admonish you
2. **Respect (v. 13a):** and to esteem them
   a) **Extent:** exceeding highly
   b) **Spirit:** in love
   c) **Reason:** for their work's sake
3. **Rapport (v. 13b):** Be at peace among yourselves

B. Responsibility of leaders to the believers (v. 14)

1. **Warning:** And we exhort you, brethren, admonish the disorderly
2. **Encouraging:** encourage the fainthearted
3. **Helping:** support the weak
4. **Forbearing:** be longsuffering toward all

C. Responsibility of saints in general (v. 15)

1. **No retaliation:** See that none render unto any one evil for evil
2. **Positive benefaction:** but always follow after

that which is good
- **a) For believers:** one toward another
- **b) For outsiders:** and toward all

D. Responsibility of Christians in their personal lives (vv. 16-18)
1. **Rejoicing always (v. 16):** Rejoice always
2. **Praying unceasingly (v. 17):** pray without ceasing
3. **Giving thanks in everything (v. 18a):** in everything give thanks
4. **Thus obeying God's will (v. 18b):** for this is the will of God in Christ Jesus to you-ward.

E. Responsibility of believers in the assembly (vv. 19-22)
1. **Quench not (v. 19):** Quench not the Spirit
2. **Despise not (v. 20):** despise not prophesyings
3. **Test everything (v. 21a):** prove all things
4. **Retain the good (v. 21b):** hold fast that which is good
5. **Reject the evil (v. 22):** abstain from every form of evil

5:12 Perhaps the elders of the church in Thessalonica had rebuked those who had quit working and who were mooching off others. And no doubt the drones didn't take the rebuke too well. That may account for this exhortation to the leaders and the led.

When Paul beseeches the saints to know those who labor among them, he means to recognize, respect, and obey their spiritual guides. This is clear from the two clauses that follow: "and are over you in the Lord, and admonish you." Elders are under-shepherds of God's sheep. Their responsibility is to teach, rule, and warn.

This verse is one of many in the New Testament that shows that there was no one-man rule in the apostolic churches. There was a group of elders in each assembly, pastoring the local flock. "At Thessalonica there was not a single president, a minister in our sense, possessing to a certain extent an exclusive responsibility; the presidence was in the hands of a plurality of men'' (Denney). However, the absence of one-man rule does not justify everyman rule. The assembly is not a democracy.

5:13 Elders serve as representatives of the Lord. Their work is the work of God. For that reason, they should be held in high regard and love.

The exhortation ''Be at peace among yourselves'' is no incidental insertion. The number one problem among Christians everywhere is the problem of getting along with one another. Every believer has enough of the flesh in him to divide and wreck any local assembly. Only as empowered by the Spirit can we develop the love, brokenness, forbearance, kindness, tender-heartedness, and forgiveness that are indispensable for peace. A particular threat to peace which Paul may be warning against here is the formation of cliques around human leaders.

5:14 This verse seems to be addressed to the spiritual leaders of the local assembly; it tells them how to deal with problem brothers.

1. Warn them that are unruly—those who won't keep in step but insist on disturbing the peace of the church by their irresponsible behavior. Here the unruly are those who refuse to work. They are the same as those described in 2 Thessalonians 3:6-12, walking disorderly, not working, but being busybodies.
2. Encourage the faint-hearted—those who need constant exhortation to rise above their difficulties and go on steadfastly for the Lord.
   Concerning the AV translation, ''Comfort the feebleminded,'' Ockenga remarks: ''If the word meant feeble-minded we would still comfort them. They seem to gather when the gospel is preached.'' And isn't this a tribute to the gospel and to the Christian church? At least there is one sphere where they find sympathy and

love and consideration.

3. Support the weak—that is, help those who are spiritually, morally, or physically weak. Spiritual and moral support of those who are weak in the faith is probably the main idea, though we should not rule out financial help as well.

4. Be patient toward all men—show the grace of long-suffering when others tend to irritate and provoke.

5:15 Speaking now to Christians in general, Paul forbids any thought of retaliation. The natural reaction is to strike back, to return tit for tat. But the Christian should be so in fellowship with the Lord Jesus that he will react in a supernatural way. In other words, he will instinctively show kindness and love to other believers and to the unsaved as well.

5:16 Joy can be the constant experience of the Christian, even in the most adverse circumstances, because Christ is the source and subject of his joy, and Christ is in control of the circumstances. This, incidentally is the shortest verse in the Greek New Testament, even if "Jesus wept" is the shortest in the English.

5:17 Prayer should be the constant attitude of the Christian—not that he abandons his regular duties and gives himself wholly to prayer. He prays at certain regular times; he also prays extemporaneously as need arises; and he enjoys continual communion with the Lord by prayer.

5:18 Thanksgiving to God should be the Christian's native emotion. If Romans 8:28 is true, then we should be able to praise the Lord at all times, in all circumstances, and for everything, just as long as in doing so we do not excuse sin.

"The shortest, surest way to all happiness is this: Make it a rule to thank and praise God for everything that happens to you. For it is certain that, whatever seeming calamity comes to you, if you thank and praise God for it, you turn it into a blessing. Could you therefore work miracles, you could not do more for yourself than by this thankful spirit: for it needs not a word spoken, and turns all that it touches into happiness'' (selected).

These three good habits have been called the standing orders of the church. They represent the will of God in Christ Jesus for us. The words "in Christ Jesus" remind us that He taught us these things during His earthly ministry and He was the living embodiment of what He taught. By teaching and example, He revealed to us God's will concerning joy, prayer, and thanksgiving.

5:19 The next four verses seem to deal with behavior in the assembly.

To quench the Spirit means to stifle His work in our midst, to limit Him, to hinder Him. Sin quenches the Spirit. Traditions quench Him. Man-made rules and regulations in public worship quench Him. A mechanical order of service quenches Him. Disunity quenches Him. "Cold looks, contemptuous words, silence, studied disregard, go a long way to quench Him. So does unsympathetic criticism" (selected). Ryrie says that the Spirit is quenched whenever His ministry is stifled in an individual or in the church.

5:20 If we link this verse with the previous one, then the thought is that we quench the Spirit when we despise prophesyings. For instance, a young brother may make some inelegant statement in public ministry. By criticizing him in such a way as to make him ashamed of his testimony for Christ, we quench the Spirit.

In its primary New Testament sense, to prophesy meant to speak the word of God. The inspired utterances of the prophets are preserved for us in the Bible. In a secondary sense, to prophesy means to declare the mind of God as it has been revealed in the Bible.

5:21 We must evaluate what we hear and hold fast to

73

that which is good, genuine, and true. The standard by which we test all preaching and teaching is the Word of God. There will be abuses from time to time wherever the Spirit has liberty to speak through different brethren. But quenching the Spirit is not the way to remedy these abuses.

I think it was Dr. Denney who wrote, ''An open meeting, a liberty of prophesying, a gathering in which anyone could speak as the Spirit gave him utterance is one of the crying needs of the modern church.''

5:22 The AV here says, ''Abstain from all appearance of evil,'' but the real sense is, ''Abstain from every form of evil.'' This may mean false tongues, prophecies, or teachings, or it may mean evil in general.

Dr. A. T. Pierson points out that there are seven distinct frames of mind for the Christian in verses 16-22.

1. The praiseful frame (16). Finding all God's dealings to be infinitely grand.
2. The prayerful frame (17). Prayer should never be unsuitable or unseemly.
3. The thankful frame (18). Even in circumstances not pleasant to the flesh.
4. The spiritual frame (19). He should have full liberty in and through us.
5. The teachable frame (20). *Any* channel which God chooses to use.
6. The judicial frame (21). Compare 1 John 4:1. Test all by the Word of God.
7. The hallowed frame (22). If evil takes shape in your mind, avoid it.

XVII. FINAL GREETINGS TO THE THESSALONIANS (5:23-28)
A. The parting petition (v. 23a)
1. Sanctification
a) **The Source:** And the God of peace himself
b) **The scope:** sanctify you wholly

74

2. Preservation (v. 23b,24)
    a) The complete person (v. 23b): and may your spirit and soul and body
    b) Complete preservation (v. 23c): be preserved entire
    c) The coveted verdict (v. 23d): without blame
    d) The coming review (v. 23e): at the coming of our Lord Jesus Christ
    e) The call of our faithful God (v. 24a): Faithful is he that calleth you
    f) The certainty of fulfillment (v. 24b): who will also do it
B. The plea for prayer (v. 25): Brethren, pray for us
C. The holy kiss (v. 26): Salute all the brethren with a holy kiss
D. The solemn charge (v. 27): I adjure you by the Lord that this epistle be read unto all the brethren
E. The gracious farewell (v. 28): The grace of our Lord Jesus Christ be with you

5:23 Now Paul prays for the sanctification of the Christians. The Source is the God of peace. The scope is found in the word "wholly," meaning "every part of your being."

There are four phases of sanctification in the New Testament—pre-conversion, positional, practical or progressive, and perfect.

Even before a person is saved, he is set apart in a position of external privilege. Thus we read in 1 Corinthians 7:14 that an unbelieving husband is sanctified by his believing wife. This is pre-conversion sanctification.

Whenever a person is born again, he is positionally sanctified by virtue of his union with Christ. This means that he is set apart to God from the world. It is referred to in such passages as Acts 26:18; 1 Corinthians 1:2; 6:11; Hebrews 10:10,14.

But then there is progressive sanctification. This is a

present setting apart of the believer to God from the world, sin, and self. It is the process by which he becomes more Christlike. This is the sanctification which Paul prays for the Thessalonians here. It is also found in 1 Thessalonians 4:3,4; 2 Thessalonians 2:13; 2 Timothy 2:21. It is brought about by the Holy Spirit when we are obedient to the Word of God (John 17:17; 2 Cor. 3:18).

Practical sanctification is a process that should continue as long as the believer is on earth. He will never achieve perfection or sinlessness on earth, but he should ever be pressing toward that goal.

Perfect sanctification refers to the believer's final condition in heaven. When he goes to be with the Lord, he will be morally like the Lord, completely and finally set apart from sin (1 John 3:1-3).

This verse has been pressed into service by some to prove the "holiness" doctrine of entire sanctification. This means that a believer can become sinlessly perfect in this life. However, that is not what Paul means when he prays, "the God of peace himself sanctify you wholly." He is not praying for the eradication of the sin nature but rather that sanctification would extend to every part of their being— spirit, soul, and body.

The apostle also prays for the preservation of the Thessalonians. This preservation should include the complete person—spirit, soul, and body. Notice the order. Man always says body, soul, and spirit. God always says spirit, soul, and body. In the original creation, the spirit was of first importance, the body last. Sin reversed the order; man lives for the body and neglects the spirit. When we pray for one another, we should follow the order found in this verse, putting spiritual welfare before physical needs.

From this verse and others, it is clear that man is a tripartite being. His spirit is that part which enables him to have communion with God. His soul has to do with his emotions, desires, affections, and propensities (John 12:27). The body is the house in which the person dwells (2 Cor. 5:1).

All parts of man need to be preserved entire, that is,

complete and sound. One commentator has suggested the needs for preservation as follows:

1. The spirit from (a) everything that would defile it (2 Cor. 7:1); (b) everything that would hinder the testimony of the Holy Spirit to the saints' relationship with God (Rom. 8:16); (c) or prevent the worship which He seeks (John 4:23; Phil. 3:3).
2. The soul from (a) evil thoughts (Matt. 15:18,19; Eph. 2:3); (b) from fleshly appetites that war against it (1 Pet. 2:11); (c) from contention and strife (Heb. 12:15).
3. The body from (a) defilement (1 Thess. 4:3-8); (b) evil uses (Rom. 6:19).

Some deny that the unsaved have a spirit. Perhaps they base this on the fact that they are spiritually dead (Eph. 2:1). However, the fact that the unsaved are spiritually dead does not mean that they have no spirit. It means that they are dead as far as fellowship with God is concerned. Their spirits may be very much alive, for example, as far as contact with the world of the occult is concerned, but they are dead Godward.

"Many are satisfied with a partial Christianity; some parts of their life are still worldly. The apostolic admonitions constantly prod into all the corners of our nature so that none may escape purification" (Lenski).

The prayer goes on to desire that God's sanctification and preservation will so extend to every part of their personalities that the believers will be without blame at the coming of our Lord Jesus Christ. This seems to point to the judgment seat of Christ, which follows the rapture. At that time, the Christian's life, service, and testimony will be reviewed, and he will be rewarded or suffer loss.

5:24 As we learned in 4:3, our sanctification is the will of God. He has called us to eventually stand blameless before Him. Having begun this work in us, He will finish it

(Phil. 1:6). He is faithful to His promise.

5:25 As Paul closes, he asks for the prayers of the saints. He never outgrew the need for prayer and neither do we. It is a sin to fail to pray for fellow believers.

5:26 Next he asks that all the brethren be saluted with a holy kiss. At that time, this was the accepted mode of greeting. In some countries it is still customary for men to kiss men, and women to kiss women. In still other cultures men kiss the women and vice versa. But more often than not this has led to abuses and has had to be abandoned.

The kiss was not instituted by the Lord as a prescribed form of greeting, neither was it taught by the apostles as obligatory. The Bible wisely allows for other modes of greeting in cultures where kissing might lead to sexual laxness. Notice how the Spirit of God seeks to guard against such irregularities by insisting that the kiss must be *holy*.

In our culture, the handshake is a safe substitute for the kiss. But please—the handshake should have some vigor, and not be like a dead fish!

5:27 To adjure means to bind by an oath. The apostle solemnly charges the elders at Thessalonica to read the epistle to all the brethren. Two points should be noted here:

1. Paul invests the letter with the authority of the Word of God. The Old Testament was read publicly in the synagogues. Now this epistle will be read aloud in the church.
2. The Bible is for all Christians, not for some inside circle or privileged class. All its truths are for all the saints. "There is no attainment in wisdom or in goodness which is barred against any man by the gospel; and there is no surer mark of faithlessness and treachery in a church than this, that it keeps its members in a perpetual pupilage or minority, discouraging the free use of Holy Scripture, and taking care that all it con-

tains is not read to all the brethren'' (Denney).

Notice that in verses 25-27 we have three keys to a successful Christian life:

1. Prayer (v. 25)
2. Love for fellow believers, which speaks of fellowship (v. 26)
3. Reading and study of the Word (v. 27)

5:28 Finally we have Paul's characteristic greeting. He opens the epistle with grace, and now he closes it with the same theme. To the apostle Christianity was grace from beginning to end.

SECOND THESSALONIANS

INTRODUCTION

It is generally believed that this letter was written from Corinth, shortly after the first letter. Paul, Silvanus, and Timothy were still together (1:1), and Corinth is the only city where we read of their being together (Acts 18:1,5).

There were three principal reasons for another letter, even so soon after the first. The saints were being persecuted and needed to be encouraged (ch. 1). They were being misled as to the day of the Lord and needed to be enlightened (ch. 2). Some were living in idleness in view of the Lord's return and needed to be corrected (ch. 3).

With regard to the day of the Lord, the believers were fearful that they were already in it. Their fears were strengthened by false rumors to the effect that Paul himself was teaching that the day was now present. So the apostle sets the record straight.

It should be apparent that the day of the Lord is not the same as the coming of the Lord, that is, the rapture. The saints were not fearful that the Lord had come; they were fearful that they were in the tribulation, which is the first phase of the day of the Lord.

Paul had never taught that any events had to occur before the rapture. But now he teaches that before the day of the Lord begins, there will be a great apostasy, the restrainer will be removed, and the man of sin will be revealed.

For the proper understanding of this letter, nothing is more important than to see the distinction between the rapture, the day of the Lord, and Christ's coming to reign. The day of the Lord is defined in the notes on 1 Thessalonians 5:2. The distinction between the rapture and the revelation is made in the commentary on 2 Thessalonians 1:7.

1

I. OPENING REMARKS (1:1,2)
  A. From (v. 1a): Paul, and Silvanus, and Timothy
  B. To (v. 1b): unto the church
    1. Its human composition: of the Thessalonians
    2. Its divine connection: in God our Father and the Lord Jesus Christ
  C. The greeting (v. 2)
    1. The two blessings: Grace to you and peace
    2. The two Blessers: from God the Father and the Lord Jesus Christ

1:1 Silvanus and Timothy were with Paul when he wrote this letter from Corinth. The letter is addressed to the "church of the Thessalonians"; this reveals its human composition and geographical location. "In God the Father" distinguishes the assembly from a heathen gathering. "And (in) the Lord Jesus Christ" marks it out as a Christian assembly.

We understand that there is still a New Testament assembly of Christians in Thessalonica (now called Saloniki).

1:2 The apostle does not wish fame, fortune, or pleasure for the saints, but grace and peace. Grace provides enablement for everything within the will of God, and peace gives serenity in every kind of circumstance. What more could a person desire for himself or for others?

Grace and peace are from God the Father and the Lord Jesus Christ. Grace precedes peace; we must know God's grace before we can experience His peace. Paul's mention of God the Father and the Lord Jesus Christ as co-sources of these blessings implies the equality of the Father and the Son.

II. PAUL'S DEBT OF THANKS (1:3-5)

A. Continual duty (v. 3a): We are bound to give thanks to God always for you, brethren

B. Appropriate duty (v. 3b): even as it is meet

C. Enlarging faith (v. 3c): for that your faith groweth exceedingly

D. Expanding love (v. 3d): and the love of each one of you all toward one another aboundeth

E. Proud acknowledgment (v. 4): so that we ourselves glory in you in the churches of God

   1. Their triumph: for your patience and faith

   2. Their trials: in all your persecutions and in the afflictions which ye endure

F. Steadfast endurance (v. 5)

   1. A token of God's justice: which is a manifest token of the righteous judgment of God

   2. A pledge of coming reward: to the end that ye may be counted worthy of the kingdom of God, for which ye also suffer

1:3 The letter begins with thanksgiving for the saints. To read this is to listen to the heartbeat of a true servant of Christ as he rejoices over his beloved spiritual children. To him thanksgiving was a continual duty of God, and it was an appropriate duty as well in view of the faith and love of the Christians. Their faith was making astonishing strides, and each one without exception was showing more and more love to the others. This was an answer to the apostle's prayer (1 Thess. 3:10,12).

Notice the order: first faith, then love. "Faith puts us in contact with the eternal spring of love in God Himself, and the necessary consequence is that our hearts are drawn out in love to all who belong to Him" (C. H. Mackintosh).

1:4   Their spiritual progress caused Paul and his associates to boast about them to other assemblies of God. They had remained steadfast and full of faith in spite of the persecutions they were enduring. Patience here really means steadfastness or perseverance.

1:5   The fact that they were standing up so bravely under the persecutions and afflictions was an indication of the just dealings of God. He was supporting them, strengthening them, encouraging them. If they had not received His divine power, they would never have been able to demonstrate such patience and faith in suffering for Christ.

Their heroic endurance proved them worthy of the kingdom of God. It did not *make* them worthy, but *manifested* them as worthy. Paul does not suggest that any personal merit entitled them to enter the kingdom; it is only through the merits of Christ that anyone will be there. But those who suffer on behalf of the kingdom here show that they are among those who will reign with Him in that coming day (Rom. 8:17; 2 Tim. 2:12).

" 'That ye may be counted worthy of the kingdom of God.' This has to do with human responsibility. On the side of divine sovereignty we have been made meet to be partakers of the inheritance of the saints in light, and this meetness is solely due to our association with Christ in His death and resurrection. We are graced in the Beloved, altogether independent of anything in ourselves, either before or since we were saved. But God allows His people to go through persecutions and tribulations in order to develop in them the moral excellencies which make them 'worthy citizens' of that kingdom. Some of the apostles rejoiced that they were counted worthy to suffer for Jesus' name. Paul's prayer for the Thessalonians that God would count them worthy of their calling most certainly had nothing to do with adding anything to the work of Christ. The Cross makes the believer worthy of his position in the kingdom, but patience and faith in tribulation manifest such an one as morally worthy of it. Among members of any earthly society there are those

83

who are discreditable as well as others. Paul prayed that it should not be so among these saints" (E. W. Rogers).

Our ability to suffer now fits us to reign in the coming kingdom. "Lifetime is training time for reigning time." Through heroic endurance we are approved as worthy to reign with Christ.

III. THE RIGHTEOUS JUDGMENT OF GOD (vv. 6–10)

A. **Recompense to the persecutors (v. 6):** if so be that it is a righteous thing with God to recompense affliction to them that afflict you

B. **Relief to the persecuted (v. 7a)**
   1. **To the Thessalonians:** and to you that are afflicted rest
   2. **To Paul and company:** with us

C. **Revelation of Christ (v. 7b)**
   1. **Arrival:** at the revelation of the Lord Jesus from heaven
   2. **Attendants:** with the angels of his power
   3. **Appearance:** in flaming fire

D. **Retribution (v. 8)**
   1. **Wilfully ignorant:** rendering vengeance to them that know not God
   2. **Wilfully disobedient:** and to them that obey not the gospel of our Lord Jesus

E. **Ruin (v. 9a):** who shall suffer punishment, even eternal destruction

F. **Removal (v. 9b):** from the face of the Lord and from the glory of his might

G. **Radiant return (v. 10):** when he shall come
   1. **Glorification:** to be glorified in his saints
   2. **Admiration:** and to be marvelled at in all them that believed
   3. **Inclusion:** (because our testimony unto you was believed) in that day

1:6 The righteous judgment of God is seen in two

ways—punishment for the persecutors and then rest for the persecuted.

The expression "if so be" does not express any doubt. It is an assured fact that God will reward affliction to those who afflict His people.

"God's action in allowing His people to be persecuted, and in permitting the existence of their persecutors, had a double purpose—first, to test the fitness of His people for government (v. 5); and second, to manifest the fitness of their persecutors for judgment" (Williams).

1:7 Just as God will award punishment to the enemies of His people, so He will award rest to those who suffer for His sake. The word "rest" here is a noun, not a verb.

We should not conclude from this verse that suffering saints will not obtain relief from trial until Christ comes back from heaven in flaming fire. When a believer dies, he obtains rest. Living believers will enjoy relaxation from all tensions at the time of the rapture. What this verse is saying is that when the Lord pours out judgment on His adversaries, the saints will be seen by the world to be enjoying rest.

The time of God's righteous retribution is at, or better *in,* "the revelation of the Lord Jesus from heaven with the angels of his power in flaming fire." Retribution for the ungodly and rest for believers are included in His coming. Which phase of Christ's coming is referred to here? It is clearly the third phase—the *manifestation* of His coming, when He returns with His saints to the earth.

But someone may ask, "How do you know that the rapture and the revelation are separate events?" The answer is that they are differentiated in the Scriptures in the following ways:

The Rapture	*The Revelation*
1. Christ comes to the *air* (1 Thess. 4:16,17)	1. He comes to the *earth* (Zech. 14:4).

85

2. He comes *for* His saints (1 Thess. 4:16,17).

3. The rapture is a mystery, i.e., a truth unknown in Old Testament times (1 Cor. 15:51).

4. Christ's coming *for* His saints is never said to be preceded by signs in the heavens.

5. The rapture is identified with the day of Christ (1 Cor. 1:8; 2 Cor. 1:14; Phil. 1:6,10).

6. The rapture is presented as a time of blessing (1 Thess. 4:18).

7. The rapture takes place in a moment, in the twinkling of an eye (1 Cor. 15:52). This strongly implies that it will not be witnessed by the world.

8. The rapture seems to involve the church primarily (John 14:1-4; 1 Cor. 15:51-58; 1 Thess. 4:13-18).

9. Christ comes as the bright and morning star (Rev. 22:16).

10. The rapture is not mentioned in the Synoptic Gospels, but is alluded to several times in John's Gospel.

2. He comes *with* His saints (1 Thess. 3:13; Jude 14).

3. The revelation is not a mystery; it is the subject of many Old Testament prophecies (Psa. 72; Isa. 11; Zech. 14).

4. Christ's coming *with* His saints will be heralded by celestial portents (Matt. 24:29,30).

5. The revelation is identified with the day of the Lord (2 Thess. 2:1-12, ASV).

6. The main emphasis of the revelation is on judgment (2 Thess. 2:8-12).

7. The revelation will be visible worldwide (Matt. 24:27; Rev. 1:7).

8. The revelation involves Israel primarily, then also the Gentile nations (Matt. 24:1—25:46).

9. Christ comes as the sun of righteousness with healing in his wings (Mal. 4:2).

10. The revelation is characteristic in the Synoptics but hardly mentioned in John's Gospel.

11. Those taken are taken for blessing (1 Thess. 4:13-18). Those left are left for judgment (1 Thess. 5:1-3).	11. Those taken are taken for judgment. Those left are left for blessing (Matt. 24:37-41).
12. No dating system is given for events preceding the rapture.	12. An elaborate dating system is given for events preceding the revelation, such as 1260 days, 42 months, 3½ years (see Dan. 7:25; 12:7,11,12; Rev. 11:2; 12:14; 13:5).
13. The title ''Son of Man'' is never used in any of the passages dealing with the rapture.	13. The revelation is spoken of as the coming of the Son of Man (Matt. 16:28; 24:27,30,37,39; 26:64; Mark 13:26; Luke 21:27).

Granted then that these are two separate events, yet how do we know that they do not occur at approximately the same time? How do we know that they are separated by an interval? Three lines of proof might be mentioned.

1. The first is based on Daniel's prophecy of 70 weeks (Dan. 9:25-27). We are now living in the parenthetical church age, between the 69th and 70th weeks. The 70th week is the tribulation period of seven years, otherwise known as the time of Jacob's trouble. The church is taken home to heaven before the tribulation period (Rom. 5:9; 1 Thess. 1:10; 1 Thess. 5:9; Rev. 3:10). The coming of Christ to reign takes place after the 70th week (Dan. 9:24; Matt. 24).

2. The second line of proof for an interval of time between the rapture and the manifestation is based upon the structure of the book of Revelation. In the first three chapters, the church is seen on earth. Chapters 4

through 19:10 describe the tribulation period when God's wrath will be poured out on the world that has rejected His Son. The church is never mentioned as being on earth during this period. The church is apparently taken to heaven at the close of chapter 3. In Revelation 19:11, Christ returns to earth to subdue His foes and to set up His kingdom—at the close of the tribulation period.

3. There is a third consideration which necessitates a time interval between Christ's coming for the saints and His coming with the saints. At the time of the rapture, *all* believers are taken out of the world and are given their glorified bodies. Yet when Christ returns to reign, there will be believers on earth who will not as yet have glorified bodies and who will marry and raise children during the millennium (Matt. 24:40,41; Isa. 11:6,8). Where do these believers come from? There must be a period of time between the rapture and the revelation during which they are converted.

Now to return to verse 7, we have the arrival of the Lord Jesus in power and great glory. He is attended by angels through whom His power is exerted.

The flaming fire may be a reference to the Shekinah, the glory cloud which symbolizes God's presence (Exod. 16:10). Or it may be a picture of the fiery judgment which is about to be unleashed (Psa. 50:3; Isa. 66:15). Probably it is the latter.

1:8 When God renders vengeance, it is not vindictiveness, but righteous recompense. There is no thought of "getting even" but rather of meting out the punishment which His holy, righteous character demands. He has no pleasure in the death of the wicked (Ezek. 18:32).

We may understand Paul as describing two classes that are marked out for retribution, as follows:

1. Those who know not God—those who have rejected

the knowledge of the true God as revealed in creation and in conscience (Rom. 1—2). They may never have heard the gospel.

2. Those who have not obeyed the gospel of our Lord Jesus Christ. These people have heard the gospel and have willingly rejected it. The gospel is not simply a statement of facts to be believed but a Person to be obeyed. Belief in the New Testament sense involves obedience.

Or both of Paul's descriptions may apply to one class—those who do not know God may be the same as those who have not obeyed the gospel.

1:9 They shall suffer punishment. A god who doesn't punish sin is no god at all. The idea that a God of love must not punish sin overlooks the fact that God is also holy and must do what is morally right.

The nature of the punishment is here defined as eternal destruction. The word translated eternal (*aionios*) is used 70 times in the New Testament. Three times it may mean ages of limited duration (Rom. 16:25; 2 Tim. 1:9; Titus 1:2). The other times it means eternal or endless. It is used in Romans 16:26 to describe the unending existence of God.

Destruction never means annihilation. It means loss of well-being, or ruin as far as the purpose of existence is concerned. The wineskins which the Lord Jesus described in Luke 5:37 were destroyed (same word as used here). They did not cease to exist, but they were ruined as far as further usefulness was concerned.

This passage is often used by post-tribulationists to confirm their position. They understand it to say that believers will not obtain rest and their persecutors will not be punished until Christ comes back to reign, and this is admittedly at the end of the tribulation. Therefore, they conclude that the hope of believers is the post-tribulation rapture.

What they fail to see is that the Thessalonians to whom this was written have all died and are already enjoying rest with the Lord in heaven. Likewise, their persecutors have all died and are already suffering in Hades.

Why then does Paul seem to say that these conditions will not take place until Christ returns to earth in power and great glory? The reason is this. That is when these conditions will be *openly manifested to the world*. Then the world will see that the Thessalonians were right and their persecutors were wrong. The saints will be seen enjoying rest when they return with Christ in glory. The destruction of the Lord's enemies at the end of the tribulation will be a public demonstration of the doom of all who have afflicted God's people in all ages.

It will help us to remember that Christ's coming to reign is a time of *manifestation*. What has been true all along will be unveiled for all the world to see. This is not true of the rapture.

The punishment of the wicked also includes banishment from the presence of the Lord and from the glory of His might. To perish without Him is to be without Him forever.

1:10 His coming will be a time of glory for the Lord and of amazement for the spectators.

He will be glorified in His saints, that is, He will be honored because of what He has done in and through them. Their salvation, sanctification, and glorification will be tributes to His matchless grace and power.

He will be marveled at in all those who believed. Amazed onlookers will gasp as they see what He has been able to do with such unpromising human beings.

And this will include the Thessalonian believers too, because they had received and believed the testimony of the apostles. They would share in the glory and triumph of "that day," namely, the day of the revelation of Jesus Christ.

By way of review, we might paraphrase verses 5-10 as follows: "Your patience in the midst of tribulation is very significant. In all this God is working out His righteous purposes. Your steadfast endurance of persecution shows that you are among the company of those who will share the glories of Christ's coming reign. On the one hand, God will measure out judgment to those who now trouble you. On the other hand, He will give rest to you who are now troubled, along with us also—Paul, Silvanus, and Timothy. He will judge your enemies when He comes from heaven with the angelic executors of His power in flaming fire, punishing those who are wilfully ignorant of God and those who are wilfully disobedient to the gospel. These will suffer everlasting destruction, even banishment from the Lord's face and from the display of His power, when He returns to be glorified in all believers—including you, because you did believe the gospel message we preached to you.''

IV. PAUL'S PRAYER FOR THE SAINTS (1:11,12)
A. **Accounted worthy (v. 11a):** To which end we also pray always for you, that our God may count you worthy of your calling
B. **Every desire realized (v. 11b):** and fulfil every desire of goodness
C. **Every work accomplished (v. 11c):** and every work of faith, with power
D. **Christ glorified (v. 12a):** that the name of our Lord Jesus may be glorified in you
E. **Saints glorified (v. 12b):** and ye in him
F. **Divine enablement (v. 12c):** according to the grace of our God and the Lord Jesus Christ

1:11 In the preceding verses the apostle has been describing the glorious calling of the saints. They have been called to suffer persecution, which in turn fits them for rule in the kingdom. Now he prays that their lives in the meantime will be worthy of such a high calling, and that God's mighty power will enable them to obey every impulse to do good, and to accomplish every task undertaken in faith.

1:12 The result would be twofold. First, the name of the Lord Jesus would be glorified in them. This means that

91

they would give an accurate representation of Him to the world, and thus bring glory to Him. Then they, too, would be glorified in Him. Their association with Him, their Head, would bring honor to them as members of His body.

Then Paul closes the chapter with the reminder that this prayer can be answered only by the grace of God and of Christ. Thus he concludes a marvelous explanation of the meaning and outcome of suffering in the believer's life. Can you imagine how encouraged the Thessalonians were when they read this reassuring message?

2

V. EVENTS PRECEDING AND DURING THE DAY OF THE LORD (2:1-12)
   A. Unfounded fears that the day of the Lord had come (vv. 1,2)
      1. The prior rapture (v. 1): Now we beseech you, brethren, touching the coming of our Lord Jesus Christ, and our gathering together unto him
      2. The apostle's request (v. 2a): to the end that ye be not quickly shaken from your mind, nor yet be troubled
      3. The pretended revelations (v. 2b): either by spirit, or by word, or by epistle as from us
      4. The disturbing report (v. 2c): as that the day of the Lord is now present (RV)
   B. Events prior to the day of the Lord (vv. 3-7)
      1. The apostasy must come (v. 3a): let no man beguile you in any wise: for it will not be, except the falling away come first
      2. The man of lawlessness must be unveiled (vv. 3b-5)

      a) His predominant characteristic (v. 3b): and the man of sin be revealed

      b) His destiny (v. 3c): the son of perdition

      c) His opposition to all forms of religion (v. 4a): he that opposeth

      d) His self-exaltation over all forms of religion (v. 4b): and exalteth himself against all that is called God or that is worshipped

      e) His self-enthronement (v. 4c): so that he sitteth in the temple of God

      f) His self-deification (v. 4d): setting himself forth as God

      g) A parenthetic reminder (v. 5): Remember ye not, that, when I was yet with you, I told you these things?

   3. The Restrainer must be removed (vv. 6,7)

      a) The present result of this ministry (v. 6): And now ye know that which restraineth, to the end that he may be revealed in his own season

      b) The present need of this ministry (v. 7a): For the mystery of lawlessness doth already work

      c) The duration of this ministry (v. 7b): only there is one that restraineth now, until he be taken out of the way

C. The manifestation of the man of lawlessness (vv. 8-12)

   1. His revelation (v. 8a): And then shall be revealed the lawless one

   2. His destruction (v. 8b): whom the Lord Jesus shall slay with the breath of his mouth, and bring to nought by the manifestation of his coming

   3. The source of his power (v. 9a): even he, whose coming is according to the working of Satan

   4. The display of his power (vv. 9b,10a): with

all power and signs and lying wonders, and with all deceit of unrighteousness

5. **The results of his power on others (vv. 10b-12)**
   a) **Their identity (v. 10b):** for them that perish
   b) **Their failure (v. 10c):** because they received not the love of the truth, that they might be saved
   c) **Their delusion (v. 11):** And for this cause God sendeth them a working of error, that they should believe a lie
   d) **Their judgment (v. 12):** that they all might be judged
      (1) **Unbelief:** who believed not the truth
      (2) **Love of evil:** but had pleasure in unrighteousness

2:1   Paul now undertakes to correct a misunderstanding that had arisen in the minds of the saints with regard to the coming of the Lord and the day of the Lord. The saints were suffering such severe persecution that it was easy for them to think that they were already in the first part of the day of the Lord, i.e., the tribulation period. And rumors were floating around that the apostle himself believed and taught that the day of the Lord had arrived. So he must set the record straight.

A crucial question arises here in verse 1 concerning a small word (Gr. *huper*) which Paul uses. The problem is whether he is beseeching the saints ''concerning'' the coming of the Lord or ''by'' the coming of the Lord. If the first is the meaning, then the passage seems to teach that the rapture and the day of the Lord are one and the same event, since the following verses clearly deal with the day of the Lord. If the second is the meaning, then Paul is appealing to them on the basis of the prior rapture that they should not think they were in the day of the Lord. The question is debatable. We agree with Kelly when he adopts the second view by saying, "The comfort of the Lord's coming is employed as a motive and means for counteracting the uneasiness created by the false presentation that the day (of the Lord) was there." We understand Paul to be saying, "I appeal to you on the basis of the rapture that you should not fear that you are in the day of the Lord. The rapture must take place first. You will be taken home to heaven at that time and will thus escape the horrors of the day of the Lord."

The expression "the coming of our Lord Jesus Christ, and our gathering together unto him" seems to refer unmistakably to the rapture. That is the time when we will be gathered to meet Him in the air.

2:2 It should be clear that the rapture is not the same as the day of the Lord. The Thessalonians were not worried that the Lord had come; they knew that He had not. But they *were* worried that the day of the Lord had begun. The intense persecution they were enduring made them think they were in the tribulation, the first phase of the day of the Lord.

Rumors had been circulating that Paul himself had said that the day of the Lord had arrived. Like most rumors, they were very garbled. One version intimated that Paul had received the information by spirit, that is, by a special revelation. According to another report, the news had come "by word," that is, the apostle had publicly taught that the tribulation had begun. "By epistle as from us" is generally understood to refer to a forged letter, purportedly from Paul, that the day of the Lord had started. The expression "as from us" probably goes with "spirit," "word," and "letter." None of these sources were to be trusted.

According to the Authorized Version, the saints were afraid that the day of Christ was at hand. This misses the point. The day of Christ, and similar expressions, point forward to the rapture and the judgment seat of Christ (1 Cor. 1:8; 5:5; 2 Cor. 1:14; Phil. 1:6,10; 2:15,16). They did not fear that the day of Christ was at hand. That would have meant release from their sufferings.

The Revised Version is better: "as that the day of the Lord is now present." They were afraid that the day of God's wrath had begun.

2:3 Now the apostle explains why they could not be in the day of the Lord. Certain events must take place first. After the rapture, these events will begin to take place.

First of all there will be the great falling away or the apostasy. What does this mean? We can only surmise that it refers to a wholesale abandonment of Christianity, a positive rejection of the Christian faith.

Then a great world figure will arise. As to his character, he is the man of lawlessness, that is, the very embodiment of sin and rebellion. As to his destiny, he is the son of perdition; he is doomed to eternal judgment.

The Scriptures contain many descriptions of important personages who will arise during the tribulation, and it is difficult to know when different names apply to the same person. Some commentators believe that the Man of Sin will be a Jewish Antichrist. Others teach that he will be the Gentile head of the revived Roman Empire. Here are the names of some of the great rulers of the end times: the Man of Sin and Son of Perdition (2 Thess. 2:3); the Antichrist (1 John 2:18); the Little Horn (Dan. 7:8,24b-26); the King of Fierce Countenance (Dan. 8:23-25); the Prince that shall come (Dan. 9:26); the Wilful King (Dan. 11:36); the Idle Shepherd (Zech. 11:17); the Beast out of the Sea (Rev. 13:1-10); the Beast out of the Earth (Rev. 13:11-17); the Scarlet Beast with seven heads and ten horns (Rev. 17:4,8-14); the King of the North (Dan. 11:6); the King of the South (Dan. 11:40); the False Prophet (Rev. 19:20; 20:10); Gog, of the land of Magog (Ezek. 38:2—39:11), not to be confused with the Gog of Revelation 20:8 who arises *after* the millennium; and the One who comes in His own name (John 5:43).

The man of lawlessness has been given an intriguing variety of identifications down through the years. He has been equated with the Roman Catholic Church, the Pope, the Roman Empire, the final form of apostate Christendom, Judas reincarnated, Nero reincarnated, the Jewish State, Mohammed, Luther, Napoleon, Mussolini, and the embodiment of Satan.

2:4 He will violently oppose every form of divine worship and will enthrone himself in the temple of God in Jerusalem, claiming to be God and demanding worship as God. This description clearly identifies him as Antichrist, the one who is opposed to Christ and who sets himself up in the place of Christ.

We learn from Daniel 9:27 and Matthew 24:15 that this blasphemous action of the Antichrist takes place in the middle of the tribulation period. Those who refuse to worship him will be persecuted and many will be martyred.

2:5 Paul used to tell the Thessalonians these things when he was with them. However, with contradictory teaching being given to them which seemed to accurately describe the fierce persecutions they were enduring, they had forgotten what the apostle had said. We all forget too easily and need to be constantly reminded of the great truths of the faith.

2:6 They knew what was restraining the full and open manifestation of the man of lawlessness, and what would continue to restrain him until the appointed time.

This brings us to the third great unanswered question in this chapter. The first is, "What is the apostasy?" The second is, "Who is the man of lawlessness?" The third is, "What or who is the restrainer?"

In the first part of verse 6, the restrainer is described in an impersonal way—"that which restraineth." But then in verse 7 he is a person—"there is one that restraineth now." "It is Something and Someone who wittingly, purposefully, and designedly holds it in check *with the view* to ensuring that the Man of Lawlessness is revealed in his own proper time" (E. W. Rogers).

Seven of the more common views as to the identity of the restrainer are: the Roman Empire; the Jewish State; Satan; the principle of law and order as found in human government; God; the Holy Spirit; and the Church indwelt by the Spirit.

The Holy Spirit seems to fit the description of the restrainer more completely and accurately than any of the others. Just as the restrainer is spoken of as Something and Someone in this chapter, so the Spirit is spoken of in John 14:26; 15:26; 16:8,13,14 as both neuter (the Holy Ghost) and masculine (He). As early as Genesis 6:3, the Holy Spirit is spoken of in connection with the restraint of evil. Then later He is seen in this same role in Isaiah 59:19b, John 16:7-11 and 1 John 4:4,

It is by the indwelling Spirit that believers are the salt of the earth (Matt. 5:13) and the light of the world (Matt. 5:14). Salt both preserves and hinders the spread of corruption. Light dispels darkness, the sphere in which men love to perform their evil deeds (John 3:19). When the Holy Spirit leaves the world as the permanent Indweller of the church (1 Cor. 3:16) and of individual believers (1 Cor. 6:19), the restraint of lawlessness will be gone.

2:7 Even when Paul wrote, the mystery of iniquity was already at work. By this we understand that a tremendous spirit of disobedience to God was already stirring beneath the surface. It was at work in mystery form—not that it was mysterious but rather that it was not yet fully manifested. It was still in germ form.

What has hindered the full display of this spirit? We believe that the presence of the Holy Spirit indwelling the church and indwelling every believer has been the restraining power. He will continue to exercise this function until He is taken out of the way, that is, at the rapture.

But here an objection is raised. How can the Holy Spirit be removed from the world? As one of the Persons of the Godhead, isn't He omnipresent, that is, everywhere at all times? How then can He leave the world?

Of course, the Holy Spirit is omnipresent. He is always in all places at one and the same time. And yet there was a distinct sense in which He came to the earth on the Day of Pentecost. Jesus had repeatedly promised that the Father and He would send the Spirit (John 14:16,26; 15:26; 16:7). How then did the Spirit come? He came as the permanent Indweller of the church and of every believer. Until Pentecost the Spirit had been *with* believers, but at Pentecost He dwelt *in* them (John 14:17). Until Pentecost the Spirit was known to depart from believers—hence David's prayer "Take not thy holy spirit from me" (Psa. 51:11b). After Pentecost the Spirit remains forever in believers of the church age (John 14:16).

The Holy Spirit will, we believe, leave the world in the same sense in which He came at Pentecost—that is, as the abiding Indweller of the church and of each believer. He will still be in the world, convicting people of sin and leading them to saving faith in Christ. His removal at the rapture does not mean that no one will be saved during the tribulation. Of course they will. But these people will not be members of the Church, but rather saved Jews and Gentiles who will be earthly subjects of Christ's glorious kingdom.

2:8 After the church has been raptured to heaven, the man of lawlessness will be revealed to the world. In this verse, the apostle skips over the career of the Antichrist and describes his ultimate doom. It almost sounds as if he will be destroyed as soon as he is revealed. But that of course is not so. He is allowed to conduct the reign of terror described in verses 9-12 before he is brought down at Christ's coming to reign.

If we are right in believing that the man of sin is revealed after the rapture and that he continues until Christ's revelation, then his mad career lasts approximately seven years—the length of the tribulation period.

The Lord Jesus will slay him by the breath of His mouth (cf. Isa. 11:4; Rev. 19:15), and will bring him to nothing by the manifestation of His coming. A word from Christ and the bright shining of His appearing are all that are necessary to end the regime of this raging impostor.

The manifestation of Christ's coming, as has already been explained, is when He returns to the earth to take the throne and reign for 1000 years.

2:9 The coming of the man of sin is in accordance with the working of Satan. His career resembles that of Satan because he is energized by Satan. He will display all kinds of miracles and signs and lying wonders.

Here it is important to note that not all miracles are of God. The devil and his agents can perform miracles. The man of lawlessness will also perform them (Rev. 13:13-15).

A miracle indicates supernatural power but not necessarily divine power. The miracles of the Lord Jesus proved Him to be the promised Messiah, not simply because they were supernatural, but because they fulfilled prophecy and because they were of such a moral nature that Satan could not have done them without harming his own cause.

2:10 The Antichrist will unscrupulously use every form of wickedness to deceive the perishing people. Who are these people? They are those who heard the gospel during the age of grace but who had no love for the truth. If they had believed, they would have been saved. But now they are deceived by the miracles of the Antichrist.

2:11 God actually sends them a working of error that they should believe a lie. The lie, of course, is the Antichrist's claim to be God. These people refused to receive the Lord Jesus as God manifest in the flesh. When He was on earth, He warned men, "I am come in my Father's name, and ye receive me not: if another shall come in his own name, him ye will receive" (John 5:43). So now they receive the man of lawlessness who comes in his own name and demands worship as God. "Light rejected is light denied." If a person sets up an idol in his heart, God will answer him according to his idol (Ezek. 14:4).

The Antichrist will probably be Jewish (Ezek. 28:9,10; Dan. 11:37,38). People would not be deceived by one posing as the Messiah unless he claimed to be descended from the tribe of Judah and the family of David.

2:12 It seems quite clear from this passage that those who hear the gospel in this age of grace but who do not trust Christ will not have another opportunity to be saved after the rapture. If men do not believe the Lord Jesus now, they will believe the Antichrist then. It says here that they *all* will be judged because of their unbelief and their love of evil. This is reminiscent of Luke 14:24, ''For I say unto you, that none of those men that were bidden shall taste of my supper.''

We know that some people will be saved during the tribulation period. One hundred and forty-four thousand Jews, for instance, will be saved and will be God's messengers in preaching the gospel of the kingdom throughout the world. Through their ministry many others will be saved. But we can only conclude that those who will be saved are those who never heard the gospel during this present age and who never deliberately refused the Savior.

VI. THE APOSTLE'S THANKSGIVING THAT THE SAINTS WOULD ESCAPE THE JUDGMENT (2:13,14)

A. **God's choice—in the past (v. 13a):** But we are bound to give thanks to God always for you, brethren beloved of the Lord, for that God chose you from the beginning unto salvation

B. **God's call—in time (vv. 13b-14a)**
   1. **Sanctification (v. 13b):** in sanctification of the Spirit
   2. **Faith (v. 13c):** and belief of the truth
   3. **Call (v. 14a):** whereunto he called you through our gospel

C. **God's consummation—in the future (v. 14b):**

to the obtaining of the glory of our Lord Jesus
Christ

2:13 In the first 12 verses, Paul had been describing the
doom of the Antichrist and his followers. Now he turns to
the Thessalonian Christians and thinks of their calling and
destiny by way of contrast. As he does so, he expresses thanks to God for these "brethren beloved of the
Lord," and proceeds to give a summary of their salvation—
past, present, and future.

"God chose you" The Bible clearly teaches that God
chooses men to salvation, but it never teaches that He
chooses some to be damned. Men are lost through their own
deliberate choice. Apart from God's intervention, all would
be lost. Does God have the right to choose some to be
saved? Basically His desire is for all to be saved (1 Tim.
2:4; 2 Pet. 3:9).

". . . from the beginning" This has two possible read-
ings. First, it may mean that God's choice was made before
the foundation of the world (Eph. 1:4). Secondly, the expression may also be read "as first fruits," indicating that
the Thessalonians, saved so early in the Christian dispensa-
tion, were chosen by God to be among the first of a great
harvest of redeemed souls.

". . . unto salvation" This should be contrasted with
the preceding verses. Unbelievers are doomed by their unbelief to eternal destruction, whereas believers are chosen to
salvation.

"in sanctification of the Spirit" Here we have the Holy
Spirit's pre-conversion work. He sets individuals apart to
God from the world, convicts them of sin, and points them
to Christ. Someone has said, "If it had not been for Christ,
there would have been no feast; if it had not been for the
Holy Ghost, there would have been no guests."

"and belief of the truth" First you have God's part in
salvation; now you have man's. Both are necessary. Some
people can see only God's election, and they imply that man
can do nothing about it. Others overemphasize man's part,

and neglect God's sovereign choice. The truth lies in both extremes. Election and human responsibility are both Bible doctrines, and it is best to believe and teach both, even if we can't understand how both can be true.

2:14 *"whereunto he called you by our gospel"* God chose us to salvation in eternity; He called us to it in time. The call refers to the moment when a person believes the truth.

The expression "our gospel" does not mean that there are other genuine gospels. There is only one gospel, but there are many different preachers of it, and many different audiences. Paul is referring to the gospel of God which was preached by him.

"to the obtaining of the glory of our Lord Jesus Christ" Here the apostle peers into the future and sees the ultimate outcome of salvation—to be with Christ and like Him forever.

> And is it so—I shall be like Thy son?
> Is this the grace which He for me has won?
> Father of glory, thought beyond all thought!
> In glory, to His own blest likeness brought!

Thus in verses 13 and 14 we have "a system of theology in miniature," a marvelous summary of the scope of God's purposes with His believing people. He has shown us that salvation "originates in a divine choice, is wrought out by divine power, is made effective through a divine message, and will be perfected in divine glory."

VII. PAUL'S APPEAL TO THE SAINTS (2:15)
   A. **Stand firm (v. 15a):** So then, brethren, stand fast
   B. **Hold fast (v. 15b):** and hold the traditions which ye were taught, whether by word, or by epistle of ours

2:15 In view of their superlative calling, the saints are exhorted to stand fast and to hold the traditions which they were taught, either by the apostles' words or by their letters. The important thing to notice here is that the only traditions which are reliable and authoritative are the inspired utterances of the apostles. Jesus condemned the scribes and Pharisees for nullifying the commandments of God by their traditions (Matt. 15:6). And Paul warned the Colossians against the traditions of men (Col. 2:8). The traditions we should hold are the great truths which have been handed over to us in the sacred Scriptures.

This verse is sometimes used to justify the traditions of churches or of religious leaders. But any traditions which are contrary to the Word of God are worthless and dangerous. If mere human traditions are accepted as equal with the Bible, who is to decide which traditions are right and which are wrong?

VIII. PAUL'S PRAYER FOR THE SAINTS (2:16,17)

    A. The Source of aid (v. 16a): Now our Lord Jesus Christ himself, and God our Father

    B. His past provision (v. 16b): who loved us and gave us eternal comfort and good hope through grace ,

    C. The needed help (v. 17)

        1. Courage: comfort your hearts

        2. Strength: and establish them in every good work and word

2:16 Having told out his message to the saints, the apostle now prays it in. He commonly follows his teaching with prayer (1 Thess. 5:23,24; 2 Thess. 3:16). The prayer is addressed to "our Lord Jesus Christ himself, and God our Father." We are accustomed to Paul's mentioning both divine persons in the same breath, but it is unusual for him to mention the Son first. He is, of course, emphasizing their essential unity and complete equality. In the Greek, the plural subject (Christ and God) is followed by four singular verb forms (loved, gave, comfort, establish). What is this but a further indication of the unity of nature of the Son and Father in the godhead?

God's past provision is introduced as an encouragement to trust Him for future courage and strength. He loved us and gave us eternal comfort and good hope through grace. Doubtless this looks back to the greatest exhibition of God's love—the gift of His Son for us. Because we know that He settled the sin question at Calvary, we have eternal consolation now and the hope of a glorious future—and it is all through His marvelous grace.

2:17 The prayer itself is that God will comfort their hearts and establish them in every good work and word. Not just encouragement in the midst of distress, but strength to move forward in the battle. The word "retreat" wasn't in the apostle's vocabulary, and it shouldn't be in ours either.

Don't miss the expression "every good work and word." In the ASV, *work* precedes *word*. The order reminds us of Acts 1:1, ". . . all that Jesus began both to *do* and to *teach*." The truth was manifest in His life before it was taught by His lips. So in our lives there should be the proper order of doing and teaching, of duty and doctrine, of practice and preaching.

3

IX. **PAUL'S REQUEST FOR PRAYER (3:1,2):**
Finally, brethren, pray for us (v. 1a)
   A. **Dissemination of the message (v. 1b):** that the word of the Lord may run
   B. **Triumph of the message (v. 1c):** and be glorified, even as also it is with you
   C. **Preservation of the messengers (v. 2):** and that we may be delivered

1. Description: from unreasonable and evil men
  2. Explanation: for all have not faith

3:1   Paul felt the need for the prayers of the saints. This chapter opens with his request for prayer in three areas:

1. For the dissemination of the message
2. For the triumph of the message
3. For the preservation of the messengers

He desires that the word of the Lord may run—a graphic picture of the gospel sprinting from place to place in spite of obstacles (see Psa. 147:15).

He also desires that the word will produce the same marvelous spiritual and moral revolutions elsewhere that it did in Thessalonica.

3:2   The third request is that the apostle and his co-workers might be delivered from unreasonable and evil men. He seems to be referring to some specific opposition, probably that which came from Jews in Corinth (Acts 18:1-18). The choice of the word "unreasonable" was appropriate; there is nothing more irrational than the opposition of men to the gospel and its messengers. It is something that baffles explanation. They may talk reasonably about politics, science, or a host of other subjects, but when it comes to the gospel, they lose all sense of reason.

X. PAUL'S CONFIDENCE CONCERNING THE SAINTS (3:3-5)
  A. **Its foundation (v. 3a):** But the Lord is faithful
  B. **Confirmation (v. 3b):** who shall establish you
  C. **Protection (v. 3c):** and guard you from the evil one
  D. **Continuation (v. 4):** And we have confidence in the Lord touching you, that ye both do and will do the things which we command

E. Sanctification (v. 5): And the Lord direct your
hearts
  1. Love: into the love of God
  2. Endurance: and into the patience of Christ

3:3 Do not miss the beauty of the contrast between
verses 2 and 3, ". . . all have not faith, But the Lord is
faithful. . . ." This teaches us to look away from faithless
men to our never-failing God. He is faithful to confirm us to
the end (1 Cor. 1:9). He is faithful to deliver us out of
temptation (1 Cor. 10:13). He is faithful and just to forgive
us our sins, and to cleanse us from all unrighteousness (1
John 1:9). And here He is faithful to establish and to guard
us from the evil one, i.e., the Devil.

"All have not faith . . . the Lord is faithful . . . we have
confidence (faith) in the Lord touching you." As Denney
has remarked, "In the Lord you may depend on those who
in themselves are weak, unstable, willful, foolish."

3:4 Now Paul reminds the saints of their responsibility
to do the things which he commands them. Here again we
have the wonderful and curious mingling of the divine and
the human: God will keep you; now you keep the commandments. It is the same thought in 1 Peter 1:5: "Kept by the
power of God" (His part), "through faith" (our part). We
also see it in Philippians 2:12,13: ". . . work out your own
salvation" (our part), "for it is God who worketh in you"
(His part).

3:5 In times of persecution it is easy to develop bitter
thoughts toward others and to give up because of the duration and intensity of the suffering. It is for this reason that
the apostle prays that the Thessalonians will love as God
loves, and will be steadfast as Christ is steadfast.

The AV "the patient waiting for Christ" is translated
"the patience of Christ" in the ASV. In the first case it
means steadfastness while waiting for Christ's return. In the
second, it means showing the same patience or endurance

which He showed as a Man on earth and which He still shows as a Man in heaven.

Some have suggested that "the Lord" in this verse is the Holy Spirit, and that therefore all three members of the Trinity are mentioned, as they are in 2:13,14.

XI. INSTRUCTIONS FOR DEALING WITH THE INSUBORDINATE (3:6-15)

A. A command to obey (v. 6): Now we command you, brethren

  1. **Authority:** in the name of our Lord Jesus Christ
  2. **Disassociation:** that ye withdraw yourselves from every brother that walketh disorderly, and not after the tradition which they received of us

B. An example to follow (vv. 7-9): For yourselves know how ye ought to imitate us (v. 7a)

  1. **Disciplined behavior (v. 7b):** for we behaved not ourselves disorderly among you
  2. **Honorable independence (v. 8a):** neither did we eat breat for nought at any man's hand
  3. **Strenuous labor (v. 8b):** but in labor and travail
  4. **Tireless industry (v. 8c):** working night and day
  5. **Unselfish consideration (v. 8d):** that we might not burden any of you
  6. **Undemanding spirit (v. 9a):** not because we have not the right
  7. **Worthy example (v. 9b):** but to make ourselves an ensample unto you, that ye should imitate us

C. A rule to remember (v. 10): For even when we were with you, this we commanded you, If any will not work, neither let him eat

D. An abuse to correct (vv. 11-15)

1. **The condition reported (v. 11):** For we hear of some that walk among you
   a) **Insubordinate:** disorderly
   b) **Idle:** that work not at all
   c) **Interfering:** but are busybodies
2. **The remedy prescribed (v. 12):** Now them that are such we command and exhort in the Lord Jesus Christ
   a) **Quietly occupied:** that with quietness they work
   b) **Consistently self-supplied:** and eat their own bread
3. **Positive policies for the church at large (vv. 13-15)**
   a) **Perseverance in piety (v. 13):** But ye, brethren, be not weary in well-doing
   b) **Discipline of the disobedient (v. 14a):** And if any man obeyeth not our word by this epistle, note that man
      (1) **Nature of the discipline (v. 14b):** that ye have no company with him
      (2) **Purpose of the discipline (v. 14c):** to the end that he may be ashamed
      (3) **Forbidden attitude (v. 15a):** And yet count him not as an enemy
      (4) **Proper attitude (v. 15b):** but admonish him as a brother

3:6 It seems clear that some of the saints in Thessalonica had stopped working for a living because they were so intently waiting for the Lord's return. Paul does not encourage this as a spiritual attitude, but proceeds to give definite instructions as to how to deal with such brethren.

His instructions are in the form of a command. The command is to withdraw from a disorderly brother, that is, one who does not keep in step with the others, but who refuses to work, and who sponges off others (see vv. 10,11). Believers should show their disapproval of such a brother by refusing to mingle with him socially. The offense is not serious enough to warrant excommunication from the assembly, however.

The tradition which the Thessalonians received from Paul was one of tireless industry, hard work, and self-support.

3:7 He did not abandon his tent-making just because he knew the Lord Jesus was coming again. He was indeed expecting Christ to come at any moment, but he was serving and working with the realization that the Lord might not come during his lifetime.

3:8 No one could accuse him of planting himself in someone's home and eating the food which someone else's toil had earned. He earned his own living while he was preaching the gospel. This meant long days and weary nights, but Paul was determined that he would not be a burden to others.

3:9 As a preacher of the gospel, the apostle had a right to be supported by those who were converted through his ministry (1 Cor. 9:6-14; 1 Tim. 5:18). But he preferred to forego this right in order that he might be an example of noble independence and unwearied diligence.

3:10 The Thessalonians had already been commanded not to support shirkers. If an able-bodied Christian refuses to work, he should not eat. Does this conflict with the fact that believers should always be kind? Not at all! It is not a kindness to encourage laziness. "The truest love to those who err is not to fraternize with them in their error but to be faithful to Jesus in all things" (C. H. Spurgeon).

3:11 Now the apostle uses a delightful play on words to bring out the inconsistency of the pseudo-spirituality of these disorderly brothers. His words have been paraphrased as follows:

1. We hear that there are some who don't attend to business but are busybodies.
2. . . . some that are not busy people but are busybodies.
3. . . . some that are not busy in their own business but are overbusy in other people's business.
4. . . . minding everybody's business but their own.

3:12 All such are commanded and exhorted in the Lord Jesus to work without fanfare and earn their own living. This is a good testimony and glorifies God.

3:13 Those who have been working faithfully are encouraged to press on. It is the end of the race that counts, not the beginning; so they should not grow weary in doing the right thing.

3:14 But what about a man who refuses to obey the apostle's instructions? The other Christians should discipline him by refusing to have social fellowship with him. The purpose of this discipline is to shame him for his behavior and constrain him to mend his ways.

However, this discipline is not as strong as excommunication. Here the offender is still looked on as a brother. In excommunication, he is counted as "an heathen man and a publican" (Matt. 18:17, AV).

3:15 The discipline of a believer always has in view his restoration to the Lord and to the people of God. It should not be carried out in a spirit of bitterness or enmity, but rather in Christian courtesy and firmness. He should be treated as a brother, not an enemy.

It seems strange to us today that Christians in Thessalonica were so ardently looking for the Lord's return that they abandoned their daily duties. That does not seem to be a peril to the church today! We have gone to the opposite extreme. We are so taken up with business and money-making that we have lost the freshness and thrill of the hope of His imminent coming.

XII. CONCLUSION (3:16-18)
A. The benediction (v. 16)
1. **His peace:** Now the Lord of peace himself give you peace at all times in all ways
2. **His presence:** The Lord be with you all
B. The salutation (vv. 17,18): The salutation of me Paul with mine own hand, which is the token in every epistle: so I write. The grace of our Lord Jesus Christ be with you all

3:16 This verse has been called "a peaceful close to a stormy epistle." In it Paul prays that the suffering saints at Thessalonica may know the peace of God at all times and in all ways.

The Christian is not dependent on anything in this world for his peace. It is based entirely on the Person and work of the Lord Jesus. The world cannot give it or take it away. But we must appropriate it in all the circumstances of life. "Peace is not cessation from persecution, but is the calm of heart that comes from faith in God and that is independent of circumstances."

3:17,18 At this point Paul apparently took the pen from the hand of his amanuensis (secretary) and wrote the closing salutation. He speaks of his salutation as being the token in every epistle he writes. Some have understood this to mean that Paul's own handwriting at the end of each letter proved it to be genuinely his. Others believe that the token is the characteristic Pauline benediction, "The grace of our Lord Jesus Christ be with you all" (Rom. 16:24, AV; 1 Cor. 16:23; 2 Cor. 13:14; Gal. 6:18; Eph. 6:24; Phil. 4:23; Col. 4:18; 1 Thess. 5:28; 1 Tim. 6:21; 2 Tim. 4:22; Titus 3:15; Phile. 25; and, if Paul wrote Hebrews, Heb. 13:25). From these references, we see that all his epistles end on a grace note.

CONCLUSION

The truth of the Lord's return appears in each chapter of 1 Thessalonians and in the first two chapters of the second epistle. It is the unifying theme, the golden thread in the pattern.

But we must always remember that prophecy is not designed to intrigue our intellect or challenge our curiosity. Its purpose is to exert a transforming influence on our lives.

For those who are believers, the hope of the imminent return of Christ has practical implications of vast significance.

1. It should exert a purifying influence on our lives (1 Thess. 5:23; 1 John 3:3).
2. It should burden us to pray and work for the salvation of the lost (Gen. 19:14; Ezek. 33:6; Jude 21-23).
3. It should encourage us to persevere in spite of persecution and trial (Rom. 8:18; 2 Cor. 4:17; 1 Thess. 4:18).
4. It should cause us to reduce our holdings of material possessions; their value declines as His coming approaches (see Lev. 25:8-10,14-16).
5. It should constrain us to apologize to anyone we have wronged and to make restitution where necessary (Matt. 5:23; Jas. 5:16).
6. It should inspire us to diligent service knowing that the night is coming when no man can work (John 9:4; 1 Thess. 1:9,10a).
7. It should keep us in the attitude of expectancy (Luke 12:36) and abiding in Him so we will not be ashamed before Him at His coming (1 John 2:28).
8. It should make us bold to confess Christ (Mark 8:38; Luke 9:26).
9. It should prove to be a comforting hope (John 14:1-3,28; 1 Thess. 4:18; 2 Thess. 1:7; 2 Tim. 2:12).
10. It should be an encouragement to moderation, gen-

tleness, forbearance, sweet reasonableness (Phil. 4:5).
11. It should be a motive for unity (1 Thess. 3:12,13).
12. It should encourage an other-worldly attitude (Col. 3:1-4).
13. It should be a reminder of coming review and reward (Rom. 14:10-12; 1 Cor. 3:11-15; 2 Cor. 5:10)
14. It should be used as a powerful appeal in preaching the gospel (Acts 3:19-21; Rev. 3:3).

For those who are not believers, the truth of Christ's return should lead them to repent of their sins and make a full commitment of their lives to Him as Lord and Savior. Only those who are in Christ will go to be with Him at the rapture. The rest will be left behind for judgment.

What if it were today?

APPENDIX ONE

Arguments for the Pre-tribulation Rapture.

1. The first argument is based on imminency. There are many Scriptures that indicate that Christians should be looking for the Lord to come at any time. We should be watching and waiting, not knowing the time of His coming. If the Church has to go through the tribulation, then we cannot be looking for Him to come at any moment. In fact, He could not come for at least seven years, since we are not in the tribulation now, and when it comes, it will last for seven years. The pre-tribulation view is the only one a person can hold and believe that Christ could come at any moment.

Here are some of the verses that indicate that we should be constantly looking for the Lord to come since we do not know the time of that event.

"And be ye yourselves like unto men *looking* for their lord, when he shall return from the marriage feast; that, when he cometh and knocketh, they may straightway open unto him" (Luke 12:36).

"And not only so, but ourselves also, who have the firstfruits of the Spirit, even we ourselves groan within ourselves, *waiting* for our adoption, to wit, the redemption of our body" (Rom. 8:23).

"For as often as ye eat this bread, and drink the cup, ye *proclaim* the *Lord's death till he come*" (1 Cor. 11:26). (Written to the Corinthians, this implied that the Lord might come in their lifetime.)

"For verily in this we groan, *longing* to be clothed upon with our habitation which is from heaven" (2 Cor. 5:2). (Believers will be clothed with their glorified bodies at the rapture.)

"For we through the Spirit by faith *wait* for the hope of righteousness" (Gal. 5:5). (The hope of righteousness is the coming of the Lord and the glorified body which we will receive at that time.)

"For our citizenship is in heaven; whence also we *wait* for a Saviour, the Lord Jesus Christ: who shall fashion anew the body of our humiliation, that it may be conformed to the body of his glory, according to the working whereby he is able even to subject all things unto himself" (Phil. 3:20,21).

"Let your forbearance be known unto all men. *The Lord is at hand*" (Phil. 4:5).

"For they themselves report concerning us what manner of entering in we had unto you; and how ye turned unto God from idols, to serve a living and true God;

115

and to *wait* for his Son from heaven, whom he raised from the dead, even Jesus, who delivereth us from the wrath to come'' (1 Thess. 1:9,10).

"*Looking* for the blessed hope and appearing of the glory of the great God and our Saviour Jesus Christ'' (Titus 2:13).

"So Christ also, having been once offered to bear the sins of many, shall appear a second time, apart from sin, to them that *wait* for him, unto salvation'' (Heb. 9:28).

"For yet *a very little while,* He that cometh shall come, and shall not tarry'' (Heb. 10:37).

"*Be patient therefore, brethren, until the coming of the Lord.* Behold, the husbandman waiteth for the precious fruit of the earth, being patient over it until it receive the early and latter rain. *Be ye also patient; establish your hearts: for the coming of the Lord is at hand.* Murmur not, brethren, one against another, that ye be not judged: *behold the judge standeth before the doors''* (Jas. 5:7-9).

"*But the end of all things is at hand:* be ye therefore of sound mind, and be sober unto prayer'' (1 Pet. 4:7).

"*And every one that hath this hope set on him purifieth himself,* even as he is pure'' (1 John 3:3).

"Keep yourselves in the love of God, *looking for the mercy of our Lord Jesus Christ unto eternal life''* (Jude 21). (Here the mercy of our Lord Jesus Christ is His return to take His blood-bought people home to heaven.)

116

"*I come quickly:* hold fast that which thou hast, that no one take thy crown" (Rev. 3:11).

"*Behold, I come quickly.* Blessed is he that keepeth the words of the prophecy of this book" (Rev. 22:7).

"*Behold, I come quickly:* and my reward is with me, to render to each man according as his work is" (Rev. 22:12).

"He who testifieth these things saith, *Yea: I come quickly:* Amen: come, Lord Jesus" (Rev. 22:20).

There are other texts which, while they might not refer directly to the rapture, yet add to the general impression that the coming of Christ is imminent. Throughout its history, the Church has held that the time of Christ's coming is unknown and that therefore it could occur momentarily.

"*Watch therefore: for ye know not on what day your Lord cometh.* But know this, that if the master of the house had known in what watch the thief was coming, he would have watched, and would not have suffered his house to be broken through. Therefore be ye also ready; for in an hour that ye think not the Son of man cometh" (Matt. 24:42-44).

"*But of that day or that hour knoweth no one,* not even the angels in heaven, neither the Son, but the Father. Take ye heed, *watch and pray: for ye know not when the time is.* It is as when a man, sojourning in another country, having left his house, and given authority to his servants, to each one his work, commanded also the porter to watch. *Watch therefore: for ye know not when the Lord of the house cometh, whether at even, or at midnight, or at cockcrowing, or in the morning;* lest coming suddenly he find you sleeping. *And what I say unto you I say unto all, Watch"* (Mark 13:32-37).

"So that ye come behind in no gift; *waiting* for the revelation of our Lord Jesus Christ" (1 Cor. 1:7).

"Christ Jesus, who is *about to judge living and dead"* (2 Tim. 4:1 JND).

"Little children, *it is the last hour;* and as ye heard that antichrist cometh, even now have there arisen many antichrists; whereby we know that *it is the last hour"* (1 John 2:18).

"If therefore thou shalt not watch, I will come as a thief, and thou shalt not know what hour I will come upon thee" (Rev. 3:3b).

"Behold, I come as a thief. *Blessed is he that watcheth,* and keepeth his garments, lest he walk naked, and they see his shame" (Rev. 16:15).

2. The second argument is based on the promise that the Church will be delivered from the wrath to come.

In Romans 5:9 AV, Paul says that "we shall be saved from *wrath* through Him."

First Thessalonians 1:10 describes the Lord Jesus as our Deliverer from the *wrath* to come.

In 1 Thessalonians 5:9 we learn that God has not appointed us to *wrath,* but to obtain salvation by our Lord Jesus Christ.

(The word "wrath" may refer to the wrath of the tribulation period, or it may refer to God's eternal judgment on unbelievers. In the Thessalonian epistles, the context favors the

118

wrath of the tribulation [see 1 Thess. 5:2,3; 2 Thess. 1:6-10; 2:10-12].)

3. In Revelation 3:10, Christ promises to keep His people from (Greek *ek,* meaning "out of") the hour of trial, which shall come on all the world, to try them that dwell upon the earth.

4. The structure of the book of Revelation bears out the teaching of the pre-tribulation rapture. In chapters 2 and 3 the Church is seen on earth, but after chapter 3 it is never mentioned again as being on earth. In chapters 4 and 5 the saints are seen in heaven, wearing victor's crowns. Then follows the tribulation on earth in chapters 6-19. The Church saints are already in heaven.

5. The tribulation period will not begin until the Man of Sin has been revealed (2 Thess. 2:3). But the Man of Sin will not be revealed until first the Hinderer is removed (2 Thess. 2:7,8). The Holy Spirit certainly answers to the name of Hinderer; He hinders or restrains the full development of evil as long as the Church is in the world. He will be removed as the Indweller of the Church at the time of the rapture.

In one sense the Holy Spirit always was in the world and always will be. But there was a special sense in which He came at Pentecost, i.e., as the permanent Indweller of believers and of the Church. It is in that sense that He will be removed at the rapture. This does not mean that the Spirit of God will not carry on a ministry during the tribulation. He will still convict and convert sinners. But He will not permanently indwell them and He will not incorporate them into the Church. His ministry will be comparable to what it was in the Old Testament period.

6. In 1 Thessalonians 4:18 the rapture is spoken of as a comforting prospect. The day of the Lord does not come as a comforter but as a thief in the night (1 Thess. 5:2). It is a

time of sudden destruction (v. 3) and wrath (v. 9) from which there will be no escape (v. 3). In contrast, the rapture is an ever brightening hope, not an ever frightening hope.

7. There must be an interval of time between Christ's coming for His saints and His coming with His saints. When Christ comes for His saints, *all* believers will be taken out of the world and will receive their *glorified bodies* (1 Cor. 15:51). Yet when Christ comes back to reign, there will be saved people who are still in their *natural bodies,* as is seen by the fact that they will be raising children (Isa. 65:20-25; Zech. 8:5). If the rapture and the revelation take place at the same time (the post-tribulation view), then where do these latter people come from?

There is a second reason why there must be an interval of time between the rapture and the reign. The judgment seat of Christ must take place in heaven following the rapture, when the Lord will judge the faithfulness of His saints and reward them accordingly (2 Cor. 5:10). The rewards given at this time will determine the extent of rule given to individual saints during the millennium (Luke 19:17,19). If the rapture and the coming to reign occurred simultaneously, there would be no time for the judgment seat of Christ to take place.

8. The only way the day of the Lord will overtake anyone is as a thief in the night (1 Thess. 5:2). Yet Paul distinctly states that it will not overtake believers as a thief in the night (1 Thess. 5:4). Therefore it will not overtake believers at all. Why not? Two reasons are given.

First, believers are not children of the night but of the day (1 Thess. 5:4-5). Second, God has not appointed believers to wrath (1 Thess. 5:9).

9. At the time of the rapture, believers go to the Father's house (John 14:3), not straight back to the earth, as post-tribulationists affirm.

10. The tribulation is distinctly Jewish in character. It is called the time of *Jacob's* trouble (Jer. 30:7). Note the Jewish references in Matthew 24: Judea, verse 16; the Sabbath, verse 20; the holy place, verse 15. These terms have nothing to do with the Church.

11. Several of the Old Testament types point to a pre-tribulation rapture. We do not build doctrine on types, but these types fit the pre-tribulation view.

a. Enoch, a type of the Church, was translated before the waters of God's judgment fell, whereas Noah and his family, types of the believing Jewish remnant, were preserved through the flood.

b. Lot was delivered from Sodom before the fires of judgment fell.

c. Abraham's offering of Isaac prefigures God offering His Son on Calvary. The first time Isaac is mentioned after that incident is when he went out to meet his bride and to take her back to his home. So Christ's first appearance after His ascension will be when He comes to take His bride home to heaven.

d. Elijah was translated to heaven before judgment was meted out to the wicked Jezebel.

12. The first 69 weeks of Daniel's prophecy (9:24-27) extend from the decree of Artaxerxes in 445 B.C. to the crucifixion of Christ. They have nothing to do with the Church. Why then should the Church be found in the 70th week, which is the tribulation period? (Actually the Church age occurs in an unmentioned parenthetical period between the 69th and 70th week.)

APPENDIX TWO

Arguments against the Pre-tribulation Rapture and in favor of a Post-tribulation Rapture.
(Answers to each argument are given in parentheses.)

1. The promise in Revelation 3:10 is not that saints will be saved out of the tribulation but that they will be kept through it (compare John 17:15).

> (The word translated "keep" in this verse means "keep out of" or "take out of." The preposition translated "from" [Greek, *ek*] means "out of." So the thought is not that the Church will be preserved *in* or *through* the tribulation, but that it will be kept *out* of it altogether.
>
> The same words are used in John 17:15 where Jesus prays, "I do not ask Thee to take them out of the world, but to keep them from the evil *one*" [NASB]. Plummer comments, "Just as Christ is that *in* which his disciples live and move, so the evil one is that *out* of which [*ek*] He prays that they might be kept." The prayer has been answered; believers have been kept *out of* Satan's dominion, and translated into the kingdom of God's dear Son.
>
> Revelation 3:10 does not teach that the Church will be protected *in* the tribulation but that it will be preserved *from* it.)

2. The Greek of Romans 5:3 says, ". . . *the* tribulation works patience."

> (Paul is not saying that the only time that tribulation works patience is during *the* tribulation period. His argument clearly is that the tribulation that believers undergo in this life develops patience.)

3. Christians have always been promised tribulation (John 16:33). There is no reason why we shouldn't go through it.

> (No one denies that "we must through much tribulation enter into the kingdom of God" [Acts 14:22]. But there is a vast difference between the tribulation that is the portion of every believer and the tribulation

period that awaits a Christ-rejecting world.)

4. Second Thessalonians 1:7 shows that the saints will not obtain rest until the Lord Jesus returns to earth at the end of the tribulation.

(The Thessalonians to whom this was written have already received their rest in heaven. But the doom of their persecutors and the vindication of the saints will be *manifested* to the world when the Lord Jesus returns in power and great glory.)

5. According to Acts 3:21, the heavens will hold the Lord Jesus until the times of restoration of all things, that is, the millennium.

(These words were spoken to *the men of Israel* [v. 12]. *As far as the nation of Israel is concerned,* the statement is true. It agrees with the Savior's words to Jerusalem in Matthew 23:39, "Ye shall not see me henceforth, till ye shall say, Blessed is he that cometh in the name of the Lord." That will take place at the end of the tribulation period. But the Church will have been raptured to heaven seven years earlier).

6. Psalm 110:1 says that Christ will sit at the right hand of God until all His enemies are destroyed. This will be at the end of the tribulation.

(In Revelation 20:8,9, we read of some who will be enemies of Christ at the end of the millennium—approximately 1000 years after the close of the tribulation. The right hand of God may describe a position of honor and power as well as a geographical location.)

7. In Titus 2:13, the blessed hope is the same as the glorious appearing. Therefore the rapture takes place at the

same time as the revelation. Therefore, we do not look for a pre-tribulation rapture but for Christ's coming to reign.

(This argument is based on a rule of Greek syntax called Granville Sharp's rule which says: When two nouns connected by "and" [Greek *kai*] are in the same case, and a definite article precedes the first noun but not the second, the second noun refers to the same person or thing the first noun does and is a further description of it. To give an example, the Greek of Titus 2:13 says, "the glory of our great God and Saviour Jesus Christ." The words "God" and "Saviour" are connected by "and"; they are in the same case [objects of preposition "of"]; the definite article "our" precedes "God" but not "Saviour." Therefore, according to Granville Sharp's rule, the word "Saviour" refers to the same person as "God" and is a further description of Him. This proves, of course, that our Savior, Jesus Christ, is God.

Now in the same verse, it says in the Greek, "looking for the blessed hope and glorious appearing." Thus it is claimed that, according to Granville Sharp's rule, the blessed hope is the same as the glorious appearing, and since the glorious appearing is generally understood to be Christ's coming to reign, the believer's hope is not a pre-tribulation rapture but Christ's coming in glory to the earth.

There are two answers to this. First of all, like all good rules, Granville Sharp's rule has exceptions. One is in Luke 14:23 where the Greek reads, "Go out into the highways and hedges." If the rule holds, then we must believe that highways are the same as hedges. A second exception is in Ephesians 2:20: "the foundation of the apostles and prophets." But no careful student would say that apostles and prophets are the same. A third exception to the rule is in Matthew 3:11: "He shall baptize you in [with] the Holy Spirit and fire." But the baptism in the Spirit is not the same as the baptism in fire. The first is a baptism of blessing, the second of judgment [see verse 12b].

But even supposing that the blessed hope *is* the same as the glorious appearing, what is to prevent us from looking on the rapture as Christ's glorious appearing to the Church whereas the revelation is His glorious appearing to the world. The words "apokalupsis" [revelation] and "epiphaneia" [shining forth or appearing] could refer to the rapture as well as to Christ's coming to reign.)

8. Other Scriptures which show that the believer's hope is Christ's coming to reign are: 1 Corinthians 1:7 (where "coming" should be "revelation," AV); 1 Timothy 6:14; 2 Timothy 4:8; 1 Peter 1:7,13; 4:13.

(The words "revelation" and "appearing" used in these passages apply both to Christ's coming for His saints and to His coming with His saints. First, He reveals Himself and appears to the Church, then later to the world.

But even if all the verses quoted did refer to Christ's coming to reign, it should be clear that the believer's hope embraces all the blessings of the prophetic future. We look forward to the rapture, Christ's coming to reign, the millennium, and the eternal state.)

9. The traditional hope of the Church has not been the pre-tribulation rapture. This only began in the last 100 years or so through the teaching of J. N. Darby.

(The New Testament Church was waiting for God's Son from heaven. The saints did not know when He would come so they watched for Him at any time.

Arguments directed at what any person did or did not teach are called *ad hominem* [to the person] and

125

are regarded as irrelevant to an issue. The question is
"What does Scripture teach?," not "What did so-
and-so teach?")

10. The last trump of 1 Corinthians 15:52 and the trump of
God (1 Thess. 4:16) are connected with the rapture and are
the same as the seventh trumpet of Revelation 11:15. Since
the seventh trumpet sounds at the end of the tribulation
when "the kingdom of this world is become the kingdom of
our Lord, and of his Christ," the return must be post-
tribulational.

(These trumpets are not all the same. The "last
trump" is the same as the "trump of God." It an-
nounces the rapture and signals the resurrection of
believers and their translation to the Father's house. It
is the "last trump" for the Church. The seventh trumpet in Revelation 11:15 is the last in a series of judgments during the tribulation. It is the last trumpet for
unbelieving Israel and unbelieving Gentiles. The
"last trump" of 1 Corinthians 15:52, also called the
"trump of God" [1 Thess. 4:16], takes place before
the tribulation. The seventh trumpet takes place at the
end of the tribulation.)

11. The first resurrection of Revelation 20:4,5 takes place
at the end of the tribulation, and not seven years earlier, as
the pre-tribulationists state.

(The first resurrection is not an isolated event but a
series. It began with the resurrection of Christ [1 Cor.
15:23]. The next stage will be the resurrection of
believers at the rapture. The third stage will be the
resurrection of tribulation saints at the time of Christ's
return to the earth [Rev. 20:4,5]. In other words, the
first resurrection includes the resurrection of Christ
and of all true believers, no matter when they are
raised. All unbelievers will be raised at the end of the

millennium to stand before the great white throne [Rev. 20:11-15].)

12. In Matthew 13:24-30, the wheat and tares grow together until the end of the age, that is, until the end of the tribulation.

(True, but this parable is speaking of the kingdom of heaven and not of the Church. There will be true and false people in the kingdom until the end of the tribulation.)

13. The rapture couldn't be secret because there will be a shout, the voice of the archangel, and the trump of God (1 Thess. 4:16).

(The teaching that the rapture will be secret is based on the fact that it will take place in the twinkling of an eye [1 Cor. 15:52]. It will be all over before the world has a chance to see anything or to know what has happened.)

14. George Muller, Samuel Tregelles, Oswald Smith, and other noted men have held the post-tribulation view.

(The argument proves nothing. There have been great men on both sides of the question.)

15. Most references in the New Testament to Christ's coming refer to His coming to reign.

(This does not deny the truth of the rapture. Just because there are more references to heaven than to hell in the New Testament does not mean that there is no hell.)

16. The Church will not endure the wrath of God in the

tribulation, but it will endure the wrath of the Antichrist or the wrath of Satan.

(Six times in the book of Revelation the wrath of the tribulation period is identified as the *wrath of God*.

"And another angel, a third, followed them, saying with a great voice, if any man worshippeth the beast and his image, and receiveth a mark in his forehead, or upon his hand, he also shall drink of the wine of *the wrath of God*, which is prepared unmixed in the cup of his anger; and he shall be tormented with fire and brimstone in the presence of the holy angels, and in the presence of the Lamb" [Rev. 14:9,10].

"And the angel cast his sickle into the earth, and gathered the vintage of the earth, and cast it into the winepress, the great winepress, of *the wrath of God*" [Rev. 14:19].

"And I saw another sign in heaven, great and marvellous, seven angels having seven plagues, which are the last, for in them is finished *the wrath of God*" [Rev. 15:1].

"And one of the four living creatures gave unto the seven angels seven golden bowls full of *the wrath of God*, who liveth for ever and ever" [Rev. 15:7].

"And I heard a great voice out of the temple, saying to the seven angels, Go ye, and pour out the seven bowls of *the wrath of God* into the earth" [Rev. 16:1].

"And the great city was divided into three parts, and the cities of the nations fell: and Babylon the great was remembered in the sight of God, to give unto her the cup of the wine *of the fierceness of his wrath*" [Rev. 16:19].)

17. When Jesus says "I come quickly" (Rev. 22:7,12,20), it does not mean at any moment. Rather it means that His coming will be sudden.

(It is a debated point. Even if it does mean "sudden," there are still verses like Hebrews 10:37 NASB; "For yet in a very little while, He who is coming will come, and will not delay.")

18. The hinderer in 2 Thessalonians 2:6-8 is not the Holy Spirit but the Roman government or the power of God.

(This has been discussed in the notes on that passage.)

19. Christ's coming couldn't have been imminent in the apostolic days because Peter and Paul both knew that they would die (John 21:18,19; 2 Pet. 1:14,15; 2 Tim. 4:6).

(Paul sometimes spoke of himself as being alive when the Lord returns [1 Thess. 4:15] and sometimes as being among those believers who would die and be raised [Phil. 3:10,11]. That is the proper attitude for all of us. We expect the Lord to come in our lifetime, but we realize that we may die before the rapture.

   Peter believed that the end of all things was at hand [1 Pet. 4:7], and he condemned those scoffers who denied the Lord's coming by saying that "all things continue as they were from the beginning of the creation" [2 Pet. 3:4].)

20. The Lord's coming cannot be at any moment because the gospel must go out to all the world before He comes (Matt. 24:14).

(This refers to *the gospel of the kingdom* [v. 14] which will go out to all the world during the tribulation period. The terms of this gospel are, "Believe on the Lord Jesus Christ and you will be saved, and when Christ comes, you will enter the millennium with Him." It is the same way of salvation that we preach, but ours looks forward to the rapture. In other words, we say, "Believe on the Lord Jesus Christ and you will be saved, and when Jesus comes, you will go to the Father's house with Him.'')

21. Passages like Matthew 28:19,20 and Acts 1:8 speak of the gospel going out to "all the nations" and to "the uttermost part of the earth." This being so, it was not possible for the Lord to come during the lifetime of the Apostles.

(In Colossians 1:6,23 Paul states that "all the world" and "all creation which is under heaven" had heard the gospel. In Romans 10:18 the gospel is said to have gone unto the ends of the world. Of course, we understand that these passages refer to the Bible world of that time, the countries adjacent to the Mediterranean.)

22. Paul's long term missionary plans, as given in Acts 18:21; 23:11; Romans 15:22-25,30,31, show that he did not expect the Lord to come in the immediate future.

(Paul's plans were made, subject to the will of God [Acts 18:21; Rom. 1:10; 1 Cor. 4:19]. He worked as if the Lord would not come back in his lifetime, but waited and watched as if He would return at any time.)

23. Paul spoke of perilous times in the last days (1 Tim. 4:1-3; 2 Tim. 3:1-5). This presupposed a time lapse during which the Lord would not come.

(Paul also said that the mystery of iniquity was already working [2 Thess. 2:7], and John said it was "the last hour" in his day [1 John 2:18]. These men did not see any problem here that made the hope of Christ's imminent return impossible.)

24. Parables such as Matthew 25:14-30 and Luke 19:11-27 presuppose that a long period of time would elapse before

the Lord returned. Therefore the early believers could not have been looking for the Lord to come at any moment.

(Apparently the early believers did not base their doctrine on parables because they *were* looking for the rapture [1 Thess. 1:10]. But quite apart from that, the "long time" of Matthew 25:19 is indeterminate. It is too indefinite to rule out imminency. The parable in Luke teaches that the *kingdom* would not appear immediately [Luke 19:11], but this does not preclude an any-moment rapture of the *Church*.)

BIBLIOGRAPHY

Denney, James. *The Epistles to the Thessalonians*. New York: Geo. H. Doran Co., no date.

Elliot, Elisabeth, Editor. *The Journals of Jim Elliot*. Old Tappan, N.J.: Fleming H. Revell Company, 1978.

Hogg, C. F. and Vine, W. E. *The Epistles of Paul the Apostle to the Thessalonians*. Glasgow: Pickering and Inglis, 1914.

Kelly, William. *The Epistles of Paul the Apostle to the Thessalonians*. London: C. A. Hammond, 1953.

Lenski, R. C. H. *The Interpretation of St. Paul's Epistles to the Colossians, to the Thessalonians, to Timothy, to Titus and to Philemon*. Columbus, Ohio: The Wartburg Press, 1937.

Rogers, E. W. *Concerning the Future*. Chicago: Moody Press, 1962.

Ryrie, C. C. *The Ryrie Study Bible*. Chicago: Moody Press, 1978.

Strombeck, J. F. *First the Rapture*. Moline, Illinois: Strombeck Agency, Inc., 1950.

Vincent, Marvin. *Word Studies in the New Testament*. Grand Rapids: Wm. B. Eerdmans Publishing Company, 1957.

Harding Wood, G. R. *St. Paul's First Letter*. London: Henry E. Walter Ltd., 1952.